How Will It END?

Hope Beyond the Headlines

D0650461

How Will It END?

Hope Beyond the Headlines

Ralph Blodgett

Pacific Press Publishing Association
Boise, Idaho
Montemorelos, N.L., Mexico
Oshawa, Ontario

Cover: Official U.S. Navy Photograph

Copyright © 1984 by
Pacific Press Publishing Association
Printed in United States of America

Library of Congress Cataloging in Publication Data

Blodgett, Ralph H., 1940—
  How will it end?

  1. Second Advent. 2. End of the world. 3. World politics—
20th century. 4. Seventh-day Adventists—Doctrines. I.
Title.
BT886.B528   1984   236'.9   84-9559
ISBN 0-8163-0567-6

 84 85 86 87 88 89 ● 6 5 4 3 2 1

Introduction

Everyone is curious about the future. Are the world economies doomed to collapse? Is nuclear holocaust inevitable? When will World War III erupt? Which new outbreak of violence will trigger the weapons of mass destruction that will end the earth as we know it?

Is Jesus coming back to planet Earth? What is this battle between God and Satan that we hear about? Does Satan exist? Will Israel become a dominant power as earth's history draws to a close? What deceptions will Satan use to deceive many during the final days? How can we know how near we are to the end? Will there really be a day of judgment? And what about the new earth that the Bible mentions in the book of Revelation? How *will* the world end, anyway?

In the twelve chapters that follow you will discover facts about tomorrow that many have little idea exist in the Scriptures. Each chapter is dedicated to the scriptural explanation of a major event leading up to the most important event in history since the crucifixion—Christ's glorious return to redeem His people.

If you've wondered what the Bible *really* does teach about earth's final days, then *How Will It End?* is must reading for you.

Ralph Blodgett

Contents

How Will It End?— The Popular View

"It is now almost forty years since the invention of nuclear weapons. . . . I do not think our luck can hold forever."—Carl Sagan, Cornell University scientist.

On Sunday evening, November 20, 1983, 100 million Americans gathered in front of their TV sets to watch ABC's $7-million movie, *The Day After*—a television dramatization of how America might look following a nuclear exchange with the U.S.S.R.

The huge viewing audience—the largest in TV movie history—witnessed a realistic vision (within the limits of what humans can imagine and television can depict) of the impact of a nuclear strike on the residents of Lawrence, Kansas, a town of 53,000 located 38 miles west of Kansas City.

As the ABC dramatization begins, a heart surgeon and his wife watch their daughter prepare to leave home, college students register for classes at the University of Lawrence, a farm family lays plans for their oldest daughter's wedding, and an airman struggles between loyalty to his wife and duty to his country as the armed services are unexpectedly put on full alert.

Woven through the first half of the film are TV and radio news bulletins telling a story few notice at first:

East Germany blockades West Berlin, warning is met with ultimatum, Moscow begins to evacuate its citizens, and Russian troops mass near the eastern borders of the communist-bloc countries.

Suddenly, news broadcasts report that NATO armored troops have broken through the blockade, two Soviet MIG 25s have attacked the NATO building in West Berlin, and advance units of the Soviet army begin invading West Germany. Rapid escalation follows. All too soon, desperately outnumbered NATO forces fire three small nuclear devices—intended for defensive field use only—to halt the advancing Russian troops.

As news of these events reaches the residents of Kansas, people rush to supermarkets for panic buying and jam freeways to get out of town. Military personnel hurry to their posts, unlock missile code boxes, and scramble Air Force bombers into the air as the machines war lurch irreversibly forward.

Suddenly, news of the destruction of a U.S. ship in the Persian Gulf and reports of Soviet readiness to launch their huge nuclear arsenal prompt U.S. generals and advisors to adopt a "use 'em or lose 'em" attitude regarding America's vulnerable land-based missiles.

Midway through the film residents of the Lawrence area, which is shown to be peppered with Air Force Minuteman silos, feel the earth shake as American ICBMs blast aloft on their way to Russia.

In one particularly dramatic scene, a mother hanging out laundry witnesses the Minuteman missiles streaking skyward as her two small children stop playing on the lawn to stare up in open-mouthed awe.

According to the movie, it matters not who pushes what button first, the end results will be the same. Suddenly, the various characters realize the inevitable—if the Minuteman missiles are outbound, Soviet warheads must already be on their way inbound!

Moments later *The Day After* depicts the sequence of two Soviet missiles striking the Kansas City area. A little boy in a field turns toward his father, and a flash of light vaporizes them both. Through the sophisticated use of trick photography and special effects, nuclear flames engulf cars on jammed freeways in giant balls of fire.

The video effects are grisly, horrifying, wrenching. Bodies become skeletons, then vaporize in midscreen; buildings explode in flaming red shards; firestorms devour forests and concrete buildings; immense fireballs engulf everything for miles around.

The Final Hour

In the final hour of the film, people suffer from radiation exposure and die. Lawrence and other outlying cities become tombs for the walking dead—stragglers, looters, wanderers, poachers, and decaying corpses.

Every creature exposed to the contaminated air is soon dead or dying. The few medical centers still functioning at all are jammed, and except for the limited power in batteries, not even a spark of electricity can be found anywhere.*

The scenes projected of a post-apocalyptic world as envisioned by scientists and physicists is unrelentingly bleak, stark, and more depressing than anything ever before dramatized on a screen. In fact, one extraordinary sequence of 1,500 radiation-exposed people

---

*Scientists believe that the massive electromagnetic pulse generated by a midair nuclear explosion most likely would disable all electrical generators and burn out transistorized and computerized communications equipment for miles around a destroyed city.

jammed into a gymnasium near the end of the film is even more memorable than the burning of Atlanta in *Gone With the Wind*.

The film ends with a message flashed on the screen: "The catastrophic events you have just witnessed are in all likelihood less severe than the destruction that would actually occur in the event of a full nuclear strike."

Is This How It Ends?

No doubt millions of Americans watching that ABC movie wondered, *Is this how the world will end—in a global thermonuclear holocaust?*

A *USA TODAY* nationwide poll conducted a few weeks after the film's broadcast revealed that 52 percent of Americans worry that a nuclear war with the Soviet Union will eventually erupt, 46 percent fear terrorists may use nuclear weapons for blackmail, and 60 percent believe the events of 1983 made a major war more likely.—*USA TODAY,* December 27, 1983.

These views have been echoed by numerous prominent figures. Scientist Carl Sagan warns, "It is now almost forty years since the invention of nuclear weapons. We have not yet experienced a global thermonuclear war—although on more than one occasion we have come tremulously close. I do not think our luck can hold forever."—*Parade,* October 30, 1983, p. 7.

Evangelist Billy Graham adds, "For the first time in history, man holds in his hands the awesome power to destroy the entire planet in a matter of minutes."—*Star,* December 6, 1983.

Exiled Soviet dissident Andrei Sakharov, in an open letter to American physicist Sidney Drell, wrote that an "all-out nuclear war means collective suicide." Such a war could "cause man to be destroyed as a biological species and could even cause the annihilation of life on earth. If the 'nuclear threshold' is crossed, *i.e.*, if any country uses a nuclear weapon even on a limited scale, the further course of events would be difficult to control and the most probable result would be swift escalation."—*Time,* July 4, 1983.

Two U.S. senators (Sam Nunn, D-Ga., and John Warner, R-Va.) stated, "There are an increasing number of scenarios that could precipitate the outbreak of nuclear war that neither side anticipated or intended, possibly involving other nuclear powers or terrorist groups."—*U.S. News and World Report,* December 5, 1983.

And columnist Jack Anderson, in an August 14, 1983, *Parade* article titled "Can We Have a Missile Accident?" described how a routine Titan missile drill on November 19, 1980, at the McConnell Air Force Base near Wichita, Kansas, nearly became a thermonuclear disaster when the missile accidentally switched into launch sequence. (Scientists later traced the near accident to wires that should have been disconnected—but weren't—by a missile maintenance crew.)

What About False Alarms?

False alarms are another problem that many worry could precipitate an all-out war—especially in view of the fact that there have already been false alarms, twice within the seven-month period, November 9, 1979, to June 3, 1980. In both cases one of the North American Air Defense Command computers set off signals that Soviet missiles from land bases and submarines were actually in flight toward U.S. targets. Fortunately, the errors were discovered in time to call off the red alert.

Others stress that almost any minor conflict involving a country of interest to both the United States and Russia could unintentionally escalate into a major nuclear confrontation. Former U.S. Secretary of Defense, James Schlesinger, for example, warned that "a nuclear war would probably get started only by miscalculation." And another former Defense Secretary, Harold Brown, added, "Strategic war is so obviously catastrophic to all engaged in it that it is only under . . . provocation and escalation—probably from lower levels of conflict—that it has any chance of happening."—*Time,* March 29, 1982.

Unfortunately, the chronology of relations between the United States and the Soviet Union over the past forty years reveals a discouraging record. *Since the end of World War II, the Soviet Union has used military power as an instrument of foreign policy at least 190 times, and the United States has used military force more than 200 times over the same period!* These shocking facts surfaced in a Pentagon-financed study conducted in 1981 by the Brookings Institution.— *Washington Post,* March 2, 1981.

The Doomsday Exercise

Many experts wonder just what it would take to turn a minor confrontation between the superpowers into an all-out nuclear holocaust. So often has this question plagued military leaders that in March 1982, Pentagon and Strategic Air Command war-gamers staged one of the most elaborate war simulations of the past twenty years. The exercise—called the Doomsday Exercise— involved dozens of senior government officials including President Ronald Reagan and Vice-President George Bush and began innocently enough with rising tensions centering on a typical European confrontation.

The simulated superpower showdown during the five-day exercise gradually escalated into a 5,000-megaton missile attack on the American mainland and the death of the President (on the fourth day) and an all-out retaliatory strike on the Soviet Union (on the fifth day) by the surviving U.S. forces.—*Newsweek*, April 5, 1982.

While the elaborate simulation answered dozens of questions in military minds, it left one issue unanswered—How would planet Earth fare following such a war?

Fragile Balance of Power

To answer that question we must take a quick look at the type of weapons that have already turned our planet into a nuclear porcupine.

In contrast to the twenty-kiloton bomb (equal to 20,000 tons of TNT) that leveled Hiroshima and killed 70,000 persons, the typical nuclear missile warhead or bomber-dropped hydrogen bomb today is *more than 100 times* the strength of the 1945 weapons (equivalent to 1 to 2 million tons of TNT).

To comprehend the destructive power of just one such warhead, picture the results of a 1-megaton nuclear explosion over the White House (*i.e.* the explosive power of a single SSN-6 missile fired from a Soviet submarine). Detonated at about 2,000 feet above the ground, the huge fireball would reduce everything—concrete, steel, brick, et cetera—within three miles of the White House (or twenty-eight square miles) to rubble.

Beyond that, winds of 400 miles per hour—stronger than any hurricane—would blast outward, crushing brick and wood buildings, stripping bark and branches from trees, igniting clothing, hurling people and automobiles through the air. Then as the mushroom cloud rose into the sky, it would suck the ground air back again, adding to the damage. Nearly everything within a five-mile radius of ground zero (or about 78 square miles) would be severely damaged, if not destroyed. People still alive would have third-degree burns, their clothes in flames, their faces and hands charred.

And beyond that, out to eight miles from the point of impact (an additional 94 square miles) brick and wood houses would sustain moderate damage. Cars would be blown off the Capital Beltway. Burns and eye damage would occur to many exposed survivors. (See illustration.) The heat would start fires beyond the eight-mile radius, and people as far as forty miles away would be cut by glass from shattered windows.

What would it look like from the ground? A *U.S. News and World Report* article describes it with these words: "The 1-megaton weapon would produce an intense white light, followed by a moment of darkness—caused when the explosion became so intense that it was opaque to light—and then an even brighter flash. The second flash would be accompanied by a surge of heat far hotter than the breath of a blast furnace, moving outward in all directions with the speed of light. Anyone exposed to the full power of that heat in downtown Washington would be incinerated."—November 28, 1983.

So powerful are today's weapons that it has been estimated that a more-or-less typical strategic warhead of 2 megatons (equivalent to 2 million tons of TNT) packs roughly the same explosive power as all the bombs exploded during World War II—a single weapon with the destructive power of the entire second world war compressed into a few seconds of time and an area thirty miles in diameter!

Circles of Death

Effect of 1-megaton nuclear explosion over White House–

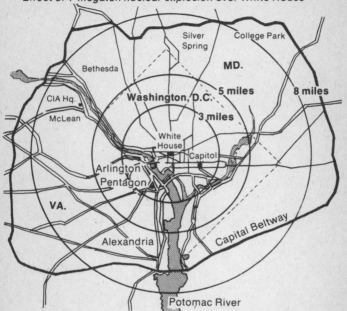

3 miles: Concrete buildings destroyed; few survivors.

5 miles: Spontaneous combustion of clothing and household items; brick, wood houses destroyed; third-degree burns or worse.

8 miles: Moderate damage to brick, wood houses; possible eye damage or burns.

How Many Such Warheads?

With these sobering thoughts in mind, ponder the fact that as of January 1, 1984, the United States and the Soviet Union together had nearly 48,000 nuclear warheads and bombs in place, ready to be delivered to their opponent's cities, industrial centers, seaports, bomber airfields, and missile-command centers. These 48,000 nuclear weapons together possess 13,000 megatons of explosive power (*i.e.*, equal to 13 *billion* tons of TNT), enough to vaporize nearly a million Hiroshimas.

Each of our nation's thirty-one Poseidon submarines carries 16 missiles, and each missile contains from 10 to 14 individually targetable warheads. That means that every Poseidon submarine carries enough firepower to level more than 200 Soviet cities. Said former President Carter in his 1979 State-of-the-Union speech, "Just one of our relatively invulnerable Poseidon submarines—comprising less than 2 percent of our total nuclear force of submarines, aircraft and land-based missiles—carries enough warheads to destroy every large and medium-sized city in the Soviet Union."—*U.S. News and World Report*, February 12, 1979.

No wonder 52 percent of Americans fear that a thermonuclear war with the Soviet Union will eventually erupt. No wonder that experts like Dr. George Wald, a Harvard University Nobel Prize-winning scientist, say, "Human life is threatened as never before in the history of this planet. . . . I am one of those scientists who finds it hard to see how the human race is to bring itself much past the year 2000."—*Countdown to Armageddon*, p. 17. No wonder that William Ogle, a retired government official who has participated in some 300 nuclear tests, warns that in a nuclear confrontation between America and Russia, "My own arithmetic says 70 percent of our population would be wiped out."—*U.S. News and World Report*, November 28, 1983.

Unfortunately the numbers of weapons and estimates of destructive force do not tell the whole picture of the results of a thermonuclear war. Not only would radioactive fallout spread for thousands of miles downwind from the attack sites, but scientists have recently concluded that the worst danger from a nuclear war would be the "pitch-dark, bone-chilling 'nuclear winter' brought on by the detonation of even less than half the megatonnage in U.S. and Soviet arsenals."—*Time,* November 14, 1983.

According to two blue-ribbon scientific studies presented to a 1983 conference attended by 600 American and foreign scientists and environmentalists, such a war would create a 1.2-billion-ton cloud of dust and smoke that would envelop both the Northern and Southern Hemispheres and block out at least 90 percent of the sun's light, plunging surface temperatures to an average of −13° F. for at least three months. During that period (even if the war broke out in midsummer), nothing could grow on earth. Everyone who survived the explosions and fallout would freeze or starve to death.—*Time,* November 14, 1983, and *Parade,* October 30, 1983.

Dr. Vladimir Alexandrov, chief of the Department of Climate Models at the Soviet Academy of Sciences, concluded, "A nuclear war of any scope would mean either the disappearance of mankind, or its degradation to a level below the prehistoric one."—*Washington Post,* December 9, 1983.

Will God Allow This to Happen?

The stark outlook for the human race in the event of a nuclear confrontation causes many Christians to wonder if God would allow humans to destroy themselves and other earth species in a thermonuclear holocaust.

Fortunately, the Bible nowhere supports the popular idea that humans will destroy themselves at the end of time. Rather it indicates that the inhabitants of the earth will be alive to witness Christ's second coming:

"Heaven departed as a scroll when it is rolled together; and every mountain and island were moved out of their places. And the kings of the earth, and the great men, and the rich men, and the chief captains, and the mighty men, and every bondman, and every freeman, hid themselves in the dens and in the rocks of the mountains. And said to the mountains and rocks, Fall on us, and hide us from the face of him that sitteth on the throne, and from the wrath of the Lamb: for the great day of his wrath is come; and who shall be able to stand?" Revelation 6:14-17.

"He cometh with clouds; and *every* eye shall see him . . . : and *all kindreds of the earth* shall wail because of him." Revelation 1:7, emphasis supplied.

The scriptures plainly declare that it will be the brightness of the Lord's return that will destroy the wicked—not nuclear missiles or hydrogen bombs: "Then shall the Wicked be revealed, whom the Lord shall consume with the spirit of his mouth, and shall *destroy with the brightness of his coming.*" 2 Thessalonians 2:8, emphasis supplied.

What About All the Weapons?

If this be the case, then why all the nuclear weapons? What part do they play in the final events?

Actually their very existence is powerful evidence that we have reached the end of time and that Christ's return is at hand.

Said Jesus to His disciples, "Ye shall hear of wars and rumours of wars. . . . For nation shall rise against nation, and kingdom against kingdom." "When ye shall see all these things, know that it is near, even at the doors. Verily I say unto you, This generation shall not pass, till all these things be fulfilled." Matthew 24:6, 7, 33, 34.

Since man now has in his hands—for the first time in human history—the awesome ability to annihilate all life on this planet in a matter of hours or days, time cannot continue much longer. Therefore, it is all the more imperative that concerned humans find out what is in store for planet Earth as history ticks out its final hours. In order to be prepared, we *need* to know how it will end, and to be reassured that there is hope beyond the gloomy headlines.

With this in mind, let's turn to the next chapter and find out how earth got into such a mess and who is behind the sin, disease, and death that we find in the world.

Does Satan Really Exist?

When police and firemen broke down the door to a five-room apartment on the first floor of a twenty-one-story building in a New York City housing project, the horrible smell of burnt flesh nearly caused them to vomit. They could hardly believe the horrifying scene that assaulted their eyes, noses, and ears as they entered.

In the middle of the room stood three people—two naked and one in a nightgown—chanting incantations beside some burning sheets and towels piled on a bed. Smoke also billowed from the kitchen, where children's clothing flamed on top of the gas stove, which had all its burners turned on full blast.

The three people they would later identify as Patricia Abraham, 25, her son Vance, 8, and Miss Abraham's mother, Lucia, 56. The clock on the wall stood at just minutes before midnight on New Year's Day.

When the firemen rushed to extinguish the flames, the younger woman pointed to the flaming bed and cried, "See the devil burn!"

As the police followed her finger, they discovered a young child writhing among the burning sheets on the bed; it was her own eighteen-month-old son, Leon.

Under all-night questioning at the twenty-sixth precinct station, Miss Abraham told the police that her son "had a fever and he looked like he was possessed."

She admitted the devil was in her as well as in her son and that she had first thrown boiling water on the boy, then placed him in the hot oven "to drive the devil out of him." The police recovered charred flesh from the oven and sent it to the police laboratory to discover whether it was human or animal flesh.

Too Awful to Believe?

If this story sounds like just the plot of another Hollywood horror film, guess again.

Two months earlier another mother, Adele Scott, 23, tossed her 4-year-old daughter out the window of a fourth-floor Brooklyn apartment. She later admitted to police that she was trying to "get rid of the devil" when she threw her child to her death on the pavement below.

Then in Wichita Falls, Texas, on February 22, 1980—less than two months after the burning of the New York child—Patricia Ann Frazier, 25, took a butcher knife and, obeying spirit voices that had invaded her mind, stabbed her 4-year-old daughter, Khunji Wilson, to death and cut out her heart. Miss Frazier was tormented by demons that had inhabited her apartment and—she thought—had taken over her daughter.

She told the police that her child's eyes had become "fishlike." "The spirits made me kill my baby," she told the court psychiatrist, Enrique Macher. All five doctors who later testified in court concurred that Miss Frazier "was unable to control herself during the attack because of the voices she believed she heard."— *The Tennessean* (Nashville), November 1, 1980.

News stories like these make my blood run cold.

First, because it's hard to believe that spirit entities—demons—can so possess a human being that a mother would burn, stab, or fling her own young child—her flesh and blood—to death. And second, because I keep hearing people say that devils don't really exist. The idea of demons, they say, was invented by superstitious humans in past ages to explain the unexplainable. We live in a scientific age, they add, and no longer follow superstitions.

Satan—Does He Exist?

Sometimes I wonder whether these people who deny Satan's existence read the same newspapers I read. How do they explain the experiences of these three mothers? How do they explain the anti-social behavior of David Berkowitz, the "Son of Sam," who snuffed out six New York residents with a .44-caliber revolver in 1977, triggering the largest manhunt in New York history? Berkowitz claimed, both then and now, that "howling demons" demanding blood directed him.

And here's another thing. If, indeed, Satan and evil beings really don't exist, then it's obvious that Bible-believing Christians have been taken in by one of the greatest shams in history. For if the devil isn't real, not only is the Bible full of lies and errors (for it talks about Satan from Genesis through Revelation), but Jesus Himself must have been deluded, for He personally *talked* with Satan in the wilderness. See Matthew 4; Mark 1; Luke 4.

No, Satan exists. He doesn't want people to believe it, but he *does* exist. Jesus Himself, warning the seventy disciples, declared, "I beheld Satan as lightning fall from heaven." Luke 10:18.

Interestingly, if Satan doesn't exist, why are more and more *non*-Christians becoming believers in him?

Why is it that people all over the world are becoming obsessed with horoscopes, astrology, parapsychology, witchcraft, tarot cards, spiritism, black magic, Ouija boards, psychic phenomena, auras, UFOs, apparitions, necromancy, necrophelia, meditation, Satan worship, and the occult?

Satan works hard on the one hand to convince Christians that he doesn't exist, while on the other hand he puts forth superhuman efforts to convince non-Christians that he is real.

According to Cassandra Salem, a witch in Orange County, California, "witchcraft seems to be growing faster right now than any other religion."—*Los Angeles Times,* May 5, 1970. In Europe satanic masses are held in ruined churches and monasteries. In Manhattan 500 witches operate, often openly, and in England 6,000 witches meet regularly in small groups. In France some 60,000 sorcerers reap $200 million a year.

"The devil's cleverest ruse," says Donald Barnhouse in his book *The Invisible War,* "is to make believe that he does not exist." Paul cautioned Christians, "lest Satan should get an advantage of us"; then added, "for we are not ignorant of his devices." 2 Corinthians 2:11.

Having answered the first of our three questions (Satan—does he exist?) positively, I would like to direct our attention to the other two important questions about Satan, namely What is he? and What is he like? Let us look at the first of these questions.

Satan—What Is He?

Let's see what the Bible says.

In Genesis, Job, and Matthew, Satan takes part in conversations with Eve, God, and Jesus, respectively. Only intelligent beings can conduct conversations of this kind, which suggests that Satan is an intelligent person.

The Scriptures describe Satan as a crafty, cunning creature (see 2 Corinthians 11:3); as one who introduces ideas into people's minds (see John 13:2, 27; Acts 5:3); as a being who aspired to be like God (see Isaiah 14:14); as the one who led out in warfare with heavenly beings (see Revelation 12:7-9); and as one who knows his time on earth is short (see Revelation 12:12). These descriptions match those of a living, thinking being, not an inanimate object or theological idea.

In 2 Corinthians 11 God's Word uses the personal pronouns *he* and *himself* regarding Satan. The Bible also employs proper names and titles for him. He is called "the prince of the power of the air" (Ephesians 2:2) and "the god of this world" (2 Corinthians 4:4). Religious leaders in Jesus' time called him "the prince of the devils" (Matthew 9:34; 12:24; Mark 3:22), and Jesus called him "the prince of this world" (John 12:31).

Satan is a distinct living being, and so are his fallen comrades. Jesus called evil beings, not good ones, "unclean spirits" and "evil spirits" in Luke 11:24 and 8:2. Furthermore, these evil spirits were originally angels in heaven who followed Satan into rebellion and sin. See 2 Peter 2:4.

How Do We Know This?

Two Old Testament passages provide a number of interesting facts about Satan's background.

The first passage—Ezekiel 28—begins with a warning against the prince of Tyrus (verses 1-10), but soon switches to the real spiritual power behind this earthly leader (verses 11-19). We know these verses refer to

Satan because they identify him as having been in the Garden of Eden (verse 13), and in God's holy mountain (verse 14), as well as having been a very high-ranking angel, or "covering cherub" (verse 16; see also Psalm 99:1).

The second passage, Isaiah 14:12-21, appears in conjunction with a message against the king of Babylon (verses 4-11), but shifts to Satan when it refers to "Lucifer," who had fallen to earth from heaven. See Luke 10:18 and Revelation 12:7-9, 12.

Now let's look at the eight facts that these verses teach about Satan.

1. *Satan originally held a high position among the heavenly host.* He was called "the anointed cherub that covereth" and had "walked . . . in the midst of the stones of fire." Ezekiel 28:13, 14. Apparently he led the heavenly host in worship and dwelt "upon the holy mountain of God," an expression in Ezekiel's time which indicated a high position in the councils of heaven.

2. *He was created perfect.* See verse 15.

3. *He was a beautiful being,* not a hooved, red-clad, goatlike creature. See Isaiah 14:12; Ezekiel 28:12.

4. *Pride led to his fall.* He wanted to "be like the most High," in other words, like God. Isaiah 14:13, 14.

5. *His activities caused a bitter struggle for power in heaven and resulted in his expulsion to earth.* See Ezekiel 28:16; Isaiah 14:15; Luke 10:18; Revelation 12:7-9.

6. *Before long he will be exposed before the whole universe for what he really is.* "I will cast thee to the ground, I will lay thee before kings, that they may behold thee." Ezekiel 28:17.

7. *Following that, God will destroy Satan with fire.* "Therefore will I bring forth a fire from the midst of

thee, . . . and I will bring thee to ashes upon the earth in the sight of all them that behold thee." Verse 18.

8. *Satan (and sin which he originated) will cease to exist permanently.* "All they that know thee among the people shall be astonished at thee: thou shalt be a terror, and never shalt thou be any more." Verse 19; see also 2 Peter 3:7, 10-13.

This brief outline of the rise and fall of the being known as Satan shows that he is an intelligent, distinct person who once was esteemed in high honor among heavenly beings. As a result of his overweening ambitions, he and his followers were cast out of heaven and came to planet Earth, where he has continued his warfare against God.

Now it's time to answer the third of our three questions, namely, What is Satan like? Again let us let the Bible be our guide as we seek to understand Satan's nature and character.

What Is Satan Like?

One way to understand Satan's nature is to examine the various names by which he is known in the Bible. This is especially important with respect to Greek and Hebrew names, since such names frequently describe the character of their possessor.

Here is a brief list of twenty different names attributed to Satan: Abaddon (Revelation 9:11); accuser (Revelation 12:10); adversary (1 Peter 5:8); anointed cherub (Ezekiel 28:14, 16); Apollyon, or destroyer (Revelation 9:11); Belial (2 Corinthians 6:15); Beelzebub (Matthew 12:24); deceiver (Revelation 12:9; 20:3, 8, 10); devil (Matthew 4:1); dragon (Revelation 12:3, 7, 9); enemy (Matthew 13:39); wicked one (Matthew 13:19, 38); Lucifer (Isaiah 14:12); murderer (John 8:44); ruler of darkness (Ephesians 6:12); Satan

(1 Chronicles 21:1); serpent (Genesis 3:4; Revelation 12:9); tempter (Matthew 4:3; 1 Thessalonians 3:5); unclean spirit (Matthew 12:43); and roaring lion (1 Peter 5:8).

What do some of these names tell us about Satan?

Devil, a name that occurs many times in the New Testament, comes from the Greek *diabolos,* meaning "one who slanders." Not only does Satan slander God and Jesus here on earth, he also slanders Christians before the whole universe.

Satan is derived from a Hebrew term that means "adversary" or "oppressor." Satan opposes God and His entire method of governing the universe.

Old Serpent reminds us of the crafty, deceitful actions of the serpent described in Genesis 3, as well as in 2 Corinthians 11:3.

Great Dragon, his title in Revelation 12, reflects Satan's warlike disposition, particularly as he led the angels in battle against the heavenly host, but also as he will attempt to attack the New Jerusalem at the end of time. See Revelation 20:7-9.

The Wicked One is how John describes Satan. See 1 John 5:18. Satan is the embodiment of evil. He is completely corrupt. He seeks to deceive and enslave as many humans as possible.

A Roaring Lion are the words Peter uses regarding Satan. See 1 Peter 5:8. What image could better convey Satan's desire to victimize and devour humans than this?

The Bible describes Satan as "a liar, and the father of it," and the "adversary" of the saints. John 8:44; 1 Peter 5:8.

Having said all this, one must be careful not to overstate Satan's power or authority. While it is true that Satan is the "prince of this world" and has a great deal of power right now, his time is limited and so is his power. Neither will continue indefinitely.

What Satan Is Not Like

Also, *Satan is not all-knowing*. If he were, he would never have permitted Jesus to die on the cross, for this act sealed his ultimate defeat. Satan is invisible. He can see us, whereas we cannot see him, but *he is not everywhere present.* The very fact that he and his angels are no longer in heaven establishes this fact. In addition it demonstrates that *Satan is not all-powerful*. John stated, "Greater is he that is in you, than he that is in the world." 1 John 4:4. And James added, "Resist the devil, and he will flee from you." James 4:7.

However, the fact that through Christ the Christian can have the mastery over Satan should never encourage anyone to walk presumptuously upon Satan's ground. Tampering with witchcraft, Satanism, and the occult, for example, has proved to be the downfall of many sincere individuals who thought they could handle Satan.

As I prepare this manuscript, I have before me newspaper articles that report that a 12-year-old boy named David Glatzel of Brookfield, Connecticut, became possessed with demons on July 2, 1980, after his sister, Debbie, 26, had playfully used a Ouija board to summon up a spirit. Subsequently demons, it seems, invaded his home.

Apparently the spirit invoked brought along many other demons. After possessing David, some of them went on to invade his friend Arne Johnson, who had commanded the demons to leave David alone. "I'm stronger than him," Arne told them; "take me on!"

Within days, according to the published accounts, Arne became possessed, and on February 16, 1981,

Arne in a sudden fit of rage allegedly stabbed to death his friend Alan Bono. Arne Johnson has since been indicted for murder. His lawyers planned to enter a defense based on demon possession—one of the first in the annals of American justice.

How Shall We Respond to Satan's Powers?

First, we must recognize that Satan is not what his fallen comrades have said he is—a hoofed, mythological creature with a pitchfork and a pointed tail. He is a fallen angel, and for a time, by the permission of God, this world is his domain. We *do* contend with *real* superhuman entities. See Ephesians 6:12.

Therefore, we must ever maintain our faith and trust in Jesus, who has absolute power and authority over Satan. When all is said and finished, Satan will have been defeated by Divinity in three major battles: first, in the battle in heaven (see Revelation 12:7-9); second, in the battle during Christ's life, ministry, and death (see John 12:31, 32); and last, when Satan is cast into the lake of eternal fire (see Revelation 20:10).

With this in mind, then, let us turn to our next chapter and examine in more detail the battle between good and evil that began in heaven and is presently continuing on planet Earth and will conclude here in the very near future. The outcome of this final battle affects virtually all of the final events scheduled to take place as time draws to a close.

The Galactic War Has Already Begun

"A long time ago in a galaxy far, far away," according to three Star Wars smash movies by George Lucas, an evil being named Lord Darth Vader came into power. This awesome, overpowering, evil personage sported a black floor-length cape, black space armor, and a grotesque breath-screen mask. He barked orders in tones that incited fear and obedience from everyone.

Darker even than his strange armor and mask were the evil intentions of this dark lord. His plans to seize control of the galaxy and to bring every creature under his corrupt control seemed irresistible.

Only a small band of faithful resistance fighters stood between Darth Vader and complete victory—people like Princess Leia, Ben Kenobi, Luke Skywalker, Han Solo, Chewbacca, and a pair of robots: C-3PO and R2-D2.

The three popular films also featured an omniscient spirit presence called "The Force." The Force, according to the movie's producer, was a supernatural power that worked only for those who believed in it enough to let it lead in their lives.

Unfortunately, evil Lord Vader also possessed supernatural powers that he had received from The Force—powers which he exercised frequently in his quest for galactic supremacy.

Based upon this good-versus-evil plot, the three films—*Star Wars* (1977), *The Empire Strikes Back* (1980), and *Return of the Jedi* (1983)—set box-office records of virtually every kind: the most ever grossed for one film ($524 million), the most ever earned in a single week ($45 million), et cetera.

Parallels With the Bible

Although billed as entertaining science-fiction films, the three Star Wars movies contained much more than just 67 million dollars' worth of mind-boggling technology, film-making wizardry, and futuristic scenarios. They contained many hints of the *true* "star war" between good and evil that is outlined in God's Word, the Bible.

One key scene on board the *Death Star* in the first movie, for example, involved Darth Vader and Ben Kenobi in hand-to-hand combat using three-foot-long light sabers. Although seemingly at a standoff, suddenly Ben dropped his guard and allowed Vader to strike him down.

His unexpected sacrifice at the last moment not only gave his friends a chance to escape but also united him with The Force. It is through his guidance from The Beyond that Luke then—against all odds—wins the final victory.

In our galaxy, the Milky Way, on our planet, Earth, something like this scenario really did happen. God sent His own Son, Jesus Christ, to engage the enemy on his own soil. Christ obtained that victory by unexpectedly sacrificing Himself, voluntarily laying down His life that we might have victory over evil, sin, and death.

God's Word has much to say about this ancient battle between "The Force" and the evil one. Let's discover for ourselves what *really* happened "a long time ago in a galaxy far, far away."

The True Story of Star Wars

The history of this great battle between good and evil takes us clear back to the beginning of life in our universe. The apostle John records the event with these words: "In the beginning was the Word, and the Word was with God, and the Word was God. The same was in the beginning with God." John 1:1, 2. A few verses later he identifies this "Word" as none other than Jesus Christ in His preincarnate form. See verses 14, 15, and 18.

John then states that "all things were made by him [the Word]; and without him was not any thing made that was made." John 1:3.

According to this text, God—working through His Son—created all forms of life in our universe. He created the angels of heaven, the beings on the other inhabited worlds of the galaxies, and the original animal and vegetable life on our small planet Earth.

"By him were all things created," states the Scripture record, "that are in heaven, and that are in earth, visible and invisible. . . . All things were created by him, and for him: and he is before all things, and by him all things consist." Colossians 1:16, 17; see also Hebrews 1:1-3.

At that point in time beautiful harmony filled the universe. Not a note of discord sounded anywhere in the hundreds of thousands of galaxies in God's creation.

Shortly, however, discontent grew in the heart of a high-ranked angel called Lucifer. He told himself, "I will ascend into heaven, I will exalt my throne above the stars of God, . . . I will be like the most High." Isaiah 14:13, 14.

Although occupying the highest position of all created beings—that of covering cherub—Lucifer wanted more. He wanted to be God.

Ezekiel provides more details of Lucifer's actions and attitudes. "Thou hast been in Eden the garden of God; every precious stone was thy covering. . . . Thou art the anointed cherub that covereth; and I have set thee so: thou wast upon the holy mountain of God. . . . Thou wast perfect in thy ways from the day that thou wast created, till iniquity was found in thee. . . . Thine heart was lifted up because of thy beauty, thou hast corrupted thy wisdom by reason of thy brightness." Ezekiel 28:13-17.

The Birth of Rebellion

Dissatisfied with his high office in the celestial government, Lucifer decided his position and physical beauty entitled him to homage and reverence from the other created beings.

When his suggestions to this effect were not accepted in the heavenly councils, he began working behind the scenes to instill doubt and discontent among the "ten thousand times ten thousand, and thousands of thousands" of angels in heaven. Revelation 5:11. He sought to undermine the authority and character of the Sovereign of the universe.

One Christian writer describes his activities thus: "Leaving his place in the immediate presence of the Father, Lucifer went forth to diffuse the spirit of discontent among the angels. He worked with mysterious secrecy, and for a time concealed his real purpose under an appearance of reverence for God. He began to insinuate doubts concerning the laws that governed heavenly beings, intimating that though laws might be necessary for the inhabitants of the worlds, angels, being more exalted, needed no such restraint, for their own wisdom was a sufficient guide.''—Ellen G. White, *Patriarchs and Prophets*, p. 37.

In order that the true nature of Lucifer's innuendos, distortions, and deceptions might be better revealed to the other inhabitants of the universe, God permitted Lucifer to continue to expand his work of discord. Before long his well-placed sparks of deceit and cunning caught fire in the dry tinder of heavenly innocence and flamed into open rebellion. ''And there was war in heaven.'' Revelation 12:7.

What Would God Do?

How could God resolve this galactic revolt? Should He simply snuff out the rebel leader and his sympathizers and create new angels to take their places? There's no doubt He had the power to do so.

And there's no doubt He would have won the battle; but in the end He would have lost the war. Love would have disappeared from His creation. For ever after, the living angels and other created beings would have shrunk from Him in fear and terror. Their worship would have risen from hypocritical hearts, their praise from joyless voices.

No, a loving God couldn't for one moment choose such a solution to the perplexing problem facing the galaxies.

On the other hand, should He capitulate to Lucifer's demands and turn over control of heaven to this proud rebellious angel? Never could the universe benefit from such leadership! That ''solution'' would have produced an eternity of disharmony and disorder.

God chose to let the universe witness the inevitable outcome of rebellion. He chose to provide an environment in which the rebellious angels could demonstrate the final result of their lawlessness. He would provide a planet on which sin could produce its inevitable harvest.

Such an example would stand as a lesson to the universe throughout all future ages, a perpetual record of the nature of sin and its dreadful results.

Hence the Scriptures record that God cast this wicked angel and his subjects down to our planet. "There was war in heaven: Michael and his angels fought against the dragon; and the dragon fought and his angels, and prevailed not; neither was their place found any more in heaven.

"And the great dragon was cast out, that old serpent, called the Devil, and Satan, which deceiveth the whole world: he was cast out into the earth, and his angels were cast out with him." Revelation 12:7-9.

Through disobedience on the part of the earth's original inhabitants (see Genesis 3:1-21), our planet became Satan's home. Thereafter, in the heavenly councils Satan represented earth as his world. See Job 1:6, 7.

Earth not only became the new battlefield; it also became the final battlefield. We have seen that Satan lost the battle in heaven. He lost the battle at Calvary some 2,000 years ago. And we have the assurance from Scripture that in the final contest for mastery over planet Earth he will also be the loser.

As you read the remaining chapters of this book, you will discover what will happen to Satan, his evil angels, and all humans who follow them in rebellion against God. In contrast, you will see portrayed the compassion of a forgiving God and His gracious offer of eternal life to all who turn to Him in faith and submission. You will also see how this greatest "star war" that the universe has ever witnessed actually ends.

Satan's Two Great Final Deceptions

> "And no marvel; for Satan himself is transformed into an angel of light." 2 Corinthians 11:14.

No book on final events would be complete without a warning about the two last great deceptions that Satan has been planning to use against the human race at the end of time.

As we have seen in the previous two chapters, Satan is a real being and is engaged in a galactic battle against good and against God's benevolent government. Earth is the battlefield for this cosmic conflict, and earth's inhabitants are the players upon which this war is focused.

Notice what the apostle John wrote in the book of Revelation after he described the war in heaven between Michael and Satan. See Revelation 12:7-11. He added, "Woe to the inhabitants of the earth and the sea! For the devil has come down to you, having great wrath, because he knows that he has only a short time." Verse 12, NKJV.

As history moves toward its final climax, Satan will escalate the level of warfare until he is fighting "with all power and signs and lying wonders, and with all deceivableness of unrighteousness." 2 Thessalonians

2:9, 10. He will do everything within his power to delude the world and to enlist as many humans as possible into his ranks of rebellion.

Satan's final game plan for planet Earth appears to focus on two methods of attack: (1) to convince humans that the dead can communicate with the living; and (2) to impersonate Jesus Christ Himself. Let's look at the first method.

Can We Talk With Dead Relatives?

The idea that the soul of man is immortal can be very comforting when a good person dies. It is encouraging to think that he lives on in another and much better world. But it isn't very comforting when a friend dies who we know wasn't fit to live in heaven. If his soul is immortal and doesn't go to heaven, it must go somewhere else. Does it go to limbo, and suffer there for years till someone's prayers and good works get him out? Or to hell to burn forever without hope? Natural immortality is not at all encouraging under these circumstances. And when we realize that maybe we ourselves may have to burn forever, the idea is positively frightening.

There is also a danger in the immortal-soul concept that you may have wondered how to avoid. If our dead relatives are still alive and can come back and talk to us, and if the devil can pretend to be someone quite different from what he really is (Paul pointed out that he can even pretend to be an angel of light), can the devil deceive us into thinking we are talking to our departed relatives when, in fact, we are communicating with evil spirits and listening to their counsel?

If it is frightening to think about burning in hell forever, it is even more unsettling to realize that the loved ones we are meeting in a séance or who write to us through a Ouija board are really agents of Satan, tricking us into accepting their advice!

Yet this is actually happening!

Paul was very concerned about this trick of Satan and said it would be increasingly common in the last days. He wrote, "The spirit speaketh expressly, that in the latter times some shall depart from the faith, *giving heed to seducing spirits, and doctrines of devils.*" 1 Timothy 4:1, emphasis supplied.

At Christ's first coming, there was a great outburst of demonic activity. Of His thirty-six recorded miracles, seven were performed to cast out demons. (See Matthew 8:28; 9:32; 12:22; 15:22; 17:15; Luke 4:35; 8:2.) So we may expect increased demonic activity just prior to our Lord's second coming.

One Christian writer described the work of Satan and his evil angels with these words:

"He has power to bring before men the appearance of their departed friends. The counterfeit is perfect; the familiar look, the words, the tone, are reproduced with marvelous distinctness. Many are comforted with the assurance that their loved ones are enjoying the bliss of heaven, and without suspicion of danger, they give ear 'to seducing spirits, and doctrines of devils.'

"When they have been led to believe that the dead actually return to communicate with them, Satan causes those to appear who went into the grave unprepared. They claim to be happy in heaven and even to occupy exalted positions there, and thus the error is widely taught that no difference is made between the righteous and the wicked. . . . With an appearance of deep interest in the well-being of their friends on earth, they insinuate the most dangerous errors. The fact that they state some truths, and are able at times to foretell future events, gives to their statements an appearance of reliability; and their false teachings are accepted by the multitudes as readily, and believed as implicitly, as if they were the most sacred truths of the Bible."—Ellen G. White, *The Great Controversy*, p. 552.

The Bishop's Son

The tragic story of the late Episcopal Bishop James A. Pike provides an appropriate illustration of this increased interest in spiritism. When the son of this Christian· minister committed suicide, the church leader so strongly believed that the dead are alive that he set out to contact his departed son.

Before long he established contact. He listened with great interest as his "son" described life in heaven in great detail. (Interestingly, the one thing the son admitted in a séance to *not* doing was seeing Jesus Christ, but he passed this off as something he would eventually be permitted to do.)

To this experience we could add many others publicized under startling headlines in the supermarket tabloids week after week.

Yet the Bible strictly condemns this type of activity: "There shall not be found among you anyone . . . who uses divination, one who practices witchcraft, or one who interprets omens, or a sorcerer, or one who casts a spell, or a medium, or a spiritist, or one who calls up the dead." Deuteronomy 18:10, 11, NASB.

God denounces such activities because He knows that the dead *cannot* communicate with the living. They are asleep in the grave (see 1 Thessalonians 4:13; 1 Corinthians 15:51, 52; John 11:11-14) and have not ascended to heaven (see Acts 2:29, 34).

The dead "sleep in the dust of the earth" (Daniel 12:2) "till the heavens be no more" (Job 14:12). Unless there is a resurrection, even "they also which are fallen asleep in Christ are perished." 1 Corinthians 15:18.

In view of these and other Bible passages,* don't let anyone tell you that he has spoken with someone who has died. You can be certain that what he talked to, no matter how convincing the conversation, was nothing more than one of Satan's demons masquerading as a departed relative or friend.

Satan's Great Final Deception

Jesus warned His followers that counterfeit Christs would appear at the end of time: "If any man shall say to you, Lo, here is Christ; or, lo, he is there; believe him not: for false Christs . . . shall rise, and shall shew signs and wonders, to seduce, if it were possible, even the elect." Mark 13:21, 22.

Although many of these counterfeits will be nothing more than humans pretending to be gods, yet it appears from Scripture that Satan, who works "with all power and signs and lying wonders, and with all deceivableness of unrighteousness" (2 Thessalonians 2:9, 10), will at the end of time impersonate Christ Himself. He will apparently pretend to be the King of the universe and will utilize "signs and wonders" to convince humans of his authenticity.

Notice how the apostle Paul warned, "and no marvel; for Satan himself is transformed into an angel of light." 2 Corinthians 11:14.

Some of his "wonders" will be genuine. The apostle

---

*For further study on what happens when a person dies, see Genesis 2:7; Job 14:12, 14, 21; Psalm 6:5; 17:15; 115:17; 146:4; Ecclesiastes 9:5, 6, 10; John 11:1-44; 1 Corinthians 15:51-54; 1 Thessalonians 4:13-17.

John tells exactly how Satan will carry out this final masquerade he will perform: "He doeth great wonders, so that he maketh fire come down from heaven on the earth in the sight of men, and deceiveth them that dwell on the earth by the means of those miracles which he had power to do." Revelation 13:13. These are not fake miracles. Men are to be deceived by the miracles which Satan will have power to do, not pretend to do. No wonder many will believe his claim to be Christ! Some think Satan will come in a UFO and land on earth as an astronaut from heaven. Others say he will just suddenly appear in various key locations around the world. However he comes, let's be on the alert!

Whatever approach he decides to use, we do know two things about this great deception: (1) the counterfeit will be so masterfully accomplished that it will "seduce, if it were possible, even the elect," and (2) that instead of appearing in clouds as Christ will when He comes, Satan will appear on earth at specific locations. See Matthew 24:23-26; Mark 13:21-23.

That's why Jesus warned, "If they say to you, 'Look, He is in the desert!' do not go out; or 'Look, He is in the inner rooms!' do not believe it. For as the lightning comes from the east and flashes to the west, so also will the coming of the Son of Man be." Matthew 24:26, 27, NKJV.

Keep in mind that miracles of themselves provide no conclusive evidence of truth. The magicians of ancient Egypt matched, at least by appearance, almost everything Moses did before the Pharaoh. See Exodus 7 and 8. So we cannot always trust our eyes or other senses to know truth from falsehood. Our only security lies in a close walk with the Lord and a knowledge of His Word.

That's also why it's so important to know exactly *how* Christ will come to this earth, so we will not be deceived by any counterfeit return that Satan might stage.

With this caution in mind, let's turn to the next chapter and answer a question asked by many concerned people regarding Christ's second coming—*Will He come secretly?*

Will Christ Come Secretly?

As our airplane pushed upward toward its assigned cruising altitude, I felt the seat pull me deeper into its grasp. Outside, the wing tip cut a path through the clouds that flashed past the window. Suddenly we broke through into clear sky, and a beam of sunlight poured warmth onto my lap.

My wife sat by the window, studying the white sea of clouds now stretched beneath us from horizon to horizon.

"Just think," I said to her, "a hundred thirty years ago our ancestors traveled the same route from the Midwest over the Rocky Mountains to the Oregon Territory—only it took them six months instead of three and a half hours."

"Times really have changed, haven't they?" she responded.

"They certainly have." I pulled the seat-control lever and eased myself into a more comfortable position. "How are the girls doing?"

She leaned forward and glanced over the top of the seat in front of us. "They're still arguing over which one gets to look out the window."

A stewardess touched me on the shoulder. "Would you like earphones, sir?"

I took the plastic sack and thanked her. As she gave

a pair to my wife, I tore open my package and removed the thin blue-plastic tubes.

I closed my eyes while the music filled my thoughts with its melody. Suddenly the plane lurched downward and banked steeply. I sat up and snatched off the earphones.

My wife was not beside me! Had I dozed off? *The "boing, boing, boing" over the speakers drew my attention to the "Fasten Your Seat Belt" sign. Seconds later, the plane leveled off and began a slow turn toward Chicago, from where we had taken off.*

Where is my wife? *I wondered.* Are my daughters all right? *I undid my seat belt and looked over the seat in front.* What? They're gone too!

Half standing, half stooping to keep from hitting my head on the storage compartment, I turned toward an elderly couple with whom my wife and I had talked a few minutes earlier. What a nice Christian couple they had seemed to be.

But when I looked, their seats were empty! "What's happening, anyway?" *I said to the two businessmen across the aisle.*

They looked up from the note-filled briefcases resting on their laps. "What do you mean?"

Before I could respond, the intercom interrupted. "This is your copilot speaking. We are experiencing an emergency situation here. Please—everyone—please sit down and fasten your seat belts. Although I cannot provide further details, it seems our captain is—ah—missing. But there is no need for alarm. I have the plane in full control, and we are returning immediately to O'Hare. Please remain calm and stay in your seats." *Before long I saw the sunlight pouring in the windows on the opposite side of the cabin.*

My wife? My daughters? The elderly couple behind

us? The captain? What is going on? Is this some kind of dream? *I glanced around.* Could I be mistaken? *"Where are the stewardesses?" I asked the two businessmen. "And weren't the seats nearly all full when we left Chicago?"*

"Why, yes," replied one. "In fact, we got the last two available."

I looked again toward my wife's seat, my children's seats, and around the plane. "Now there are empty seats all over the plane! At least thirty or forty people are missing," I said. "People don't just disappear from a plane traveling 650 miles an hour! Where have they gone?"

The Rapture Teaching

Does this story sound preposterous? Maybe so, and yet maybe not. You will find similar accounts in any number of books currently coming off religious presses. Such accounts follow a relatively new teaching called the rapture. According to this popular teaching, people by the thousands will suddenly vanish from sight—from airplanes in mid-flight, from autos on the freeways, from supermarkets, schools, factories, and even from homes behind locked doors.

What will have happened to them? According to this new teaching, they will have been "raptured" to meet Jesus Christ in the air and taken to heaven. Those left behind will not see them leave, the proponents claim, nor will they see Jesus in the sky calling His people heavenward. Why? Because this return of Christ will be His rapturous second coming.

Seven years later, though, the ones left behind will see Jesus coming again—this time with those He took away at the rapture. This return, they affirm, will be "another" second coming of Jesus.

Between these two advents—the first *for* His people, the second *with* His people—they say the antichrist will arise and persecute the Jews, who will be trying to convert the world to Christ. It will be a time of tribulation, accompanied by the seven last plagues; and then the King of the universe will return to set up His thousand-year-long kingdom of peace (commonly called the millennium).

Now, among the folk who teach this view of the second coming are many very good Christians, some of whom are very serious students of the Bible, so it would be quite irresponsible for anyone to dismiss the rapture just because it may seem a bit silly to talk about airplane passengers disappearing from their seats in mid-flight. Certainly no one should say there is nothing in the Bible to support it, because at least some texts do seem to. It would also be wrong to accept the rapture just because other people do. Each of us should study these things out for himself. Do all the texts that deal with the second coming support the rapture? Are there any texts that simply don't fit, suggesting that perhaps the rapture may not be right? One thing that especially concerns some Christians is that the rapture theory promises people a second chance. If they don't accept Christ before the rapture, they will have a second chance afterward, before Jesus comes *with* His saints.

The great danger with possible second chances is that they very often make people careless about their first chance. And if, as many believe, there really is only one chance, if a person must become a Christian before Christ comes for His saints, then putting off repentance and conversion until after the Rapture could be fatal to one's hope of eternal life.

Let me show you a few Bible texts so you can see

what I mean. First, a quick look at what the Bible teaches about Christ's second coming.

What will happen when Christ returns? Here are some of the texts in which the Bible describes the event. The Bible says that Jesus will come in this manner:

1. With His angels. See Matthew 24:31; Mark 8:38.

2. With power and great glory. See Matthew 24:30; Mark 13:26; Luke 21:27.

3. With a shout. See 1 Thessalonians 4:16.

4. With the voice of the archangel. See 1 Thessalonians 4:16.

5. With a great sound of a trumpet. See Matthew 24:31; 1 Corinthians 15:52; 1 Thessalonians 4:16.

6. In the glory of His Father. See Matthew 16:27; Mark 8:38; Luke 9:26.

7. In His own glory. Luke 9:26.

8. With all the holy angels. See Matthew 25:31.

9. With brightness. See 2 Thessalonians 2:8.

10. In flaming fire. See 2 Thessalonians 1:7, 8.

11. As the lightning shineth. See Matthew 24:27.

12. Visibly—every eye shall see Him. See Revelation 1:7.

Literally, Visibly, Personally

As Jesus came literally, visibly, and personally the first time, so also will He come the second time. As His first coming fulfilled Bible predictions to the letter, so will the second. As His shame on the cross at His first coming was literal and visible to all, so also will His glory at His second coming be visible to all.

"Behold, he cometh with clouds," John says, "and *every eye* shall see him, and they also which pierced him: and all kindreds of the earth shall wail because of him." Revelation 1:7, emphasis supplied.

The righteous will see Him return. See Acts 1:11; Hebrews 9:28. And so will the wicked. See Matthew 24:30; Mark 13:26; Luke 21:27.

He will return audibly. See Psalm 50:3; Matthew 24:31; 1 Corinthians 15:52; 1 Thessalonians 4:16.

He will return personally. See Acts 1:11.

He will return gloriously. See Mark 13:26; Luke 21:27.

He will return before the millennium. See Matthew 24:36-39, 44; 1 Thessalonians 4:15-17; Revelation 20:6.

Not a Silent Event

The Bible says that Christ's return will be neither quiet nor secret: "Our God shall come, and *shall not keep silence:* a fire shall devour before him, and it shall be very tempestuous round about him." Psalm 50:3, emphasis supplied.

The Scriptures declare that three loud sounds will accompany His return: the sound of the "shout," the sound of "the voice of the archangel," and the sound of "the trump of God." 1 Thessalonians 4:16.

The word *voice* here stems from the Greek word *phone* (pronounced "fonay"), from which we get such words as *telephone, earphone, phonograph*, and *phonics*. Of what value would an inaudible telephone be? Or an inaudible phonograph?

The people of New Testament times heard "the voice [*phone*]" of one man "crying in the wilderness" (John the Baptist: Matthew 3:3); how could the voice *(phone)* of the archangel be inaudible? The people assembled around Lazarus' grave heard Jesus when He "cried with a loud voice [*phone*], Lazarus, come forth" (John 11:43); how could "the voice [*phone*] of the archangel" at Christ's return be inaudible? The Greek word in all these passages is the same.

"The trump [trumpet] of God" will proclaim Christ's return to the inhabitants of earth. 1 Thessalonians 4:16. Of all musical instruments the trumpet is among the loudest. No inaudible instrument this!

Every inhabitant of the world will hear this "trump of God"—not just the living righteous. Look at the Scripture record: "*All* ye inhabitants of the world, and dwellers on the earth, see ye; . . . and when he bloweth a trumpet, *hear* ye." Isaiah 18:3, emphasis supplied.

Accompanying the sounds of the "shout," "the voice of the archangel," and "the trump of God" will be the noise of graves opening as "the dead in Christ . . . rise." 1 Thessalonians 4:17.

Perhaps you have loved ones laid away in the cemetery awaiting resurrection morning. Thank God that at the voice of the archangel and the trumpet of God the dead in Christ will be resurrected (see 1 Corinthians 15:22, 23, 52), then gathered together with the righteous living by God's angels (see Matthew 24:31) from the "uttermost" parts of the earth (see Mark 13:27).

At that time the righteous, with radiant faces and smiling lips, will cry out, "Lo, this is our God; we have waited for him, and he will save us: this is the Lord; we have waited for him, we will be glad and rejoice in his salvation." Isaiah 25:9.

A Second Chance

The rapture theory says that during the seven-year interlude between Christ's two second comings, God will give people another chance to be saved. You will remember that this is the aspect of the theory that gives some Christians the most concern.

Jesus said that at His second coming the righteous and wicked will be permanently separated. Note how

Matthew recorded His discourse on the subject, Matthew 25:31-46: "Before him shall be gathered all nations." Verse 32. Not just the righteous but *all* nations. "And," verse 33 says, "he shall separate them one from another, as a shepherd divideth his sheep from the goats."

To one group Jesus will say, "Come, ye blessed of my Father, inherit the kingdom prepared for you from the foundation of the world." To the other He will say, "Depart from me, ye cursed, into everlasting fire, prepared for the devil and his angels."

Christ calls this separation the "harvest" of the earth. See Matthew 13:24-30, 36-43. Note especially that in Matthew 13 the wheat represents "the children of the kingdom" and "the tares are the children of the wicked one." The householder tells his servants to "let both grow together till the harvest."

In that parable Christ did not say, "Take the wheat out secretly and let the tares continue growing by themselves for seven more years until I return." He said, "Let both grow together till the harvest." Then, when "the harvest is ripe" He will "thrust in his sickle." Revelation 14:14-20. Speaking in another place of the same event, He said, "Behold, I come quickly; and my reward is with me, to give *every* man [both good and bad] according as his work shall be." Revelation 22:12, emphasis supplied. To "every man"—not just to the righteous.

The Gap Theory

No scriptural support exists for a seven-year period between any two phases of Christ's second coming. The human race will not have another chance at salvation. God provides the world with its second chance *now*. He gave mankind its first chance in the Garden of

Eden. By God's infinite love, the world received a second chance through the sacrifice of Jesus on Calvary's cross. There will be no third chance. The Bible declares, "*Now* is the day of salvation." 2 Corinthians 6:2. "*Today* if ye will hear his voice harden not your hearts." Hebrews 4:7. "Choose you *this day* whom ye will serve." Joshua 24:15, emphases supplied. Never tomorrow. Always today, *now!*

The parable of the ten virgins (Matthew 25:1-13) verifies that there will be no later chance for those not found ready when the Bridegroom comes. According to the parable, when Christ (the Bridegroom) returns, He will accept only those found prepared to enter the banquet hall. The door once shut will be shut forever. Luke 13:24, 25 describes the tragic impossibility of another chance for anyone who is not then ready.

Those not ready to enter when the Bridegroom comes will be left outside. They will weep and bitterly regret their loss. See Luke 13:28. Jesus warned, "Then shall all the tribes of the earth mourn, and they shall see the Son of man coming in the clouds of heaven with power and great glory." Matthew 24:30.

They will cry for the mountains and rocks to fall on them and hide them from the glory of Christ's coming. See Revelation 6:14-17. They will realize that the time has come for the Son of man to reap the earth (see Revelation 14:14-19) and that they remain "filthy still" (Revelation 22:11).

At that time the living wicked, along with "that wicked" one mentioned in 2 Thessalonians 2, will be destroyed "with the brightness of his coming." Verse 8. Then the earth will be left to Satan, with "no man," animal, or bird on the world for a thousand years (the millennium). Jeremiah described this period in these words:

"I beheld the earth, and, lo, it was without form, and void; and the heavens, and they had no light. I beheld the mountains, and, lo, they trembled, and all the hills moved lightly. I beheld, and, lo, there was no man, and all the birds of the heavens were fled. I beheld, and, lo, the fruitful place was a wilderness, and all the cities thereof were broken down *at the presence of the Lord,* and by his fierce anger. For thus hath the Lord said, The whole land shall be desolate; *yet will I not make a full end."* Jeremiah 4:23-27, emphasis supplied.

Note especially the last eight words: "Yet will I not make a full end." The final destruction of the wicked is yet to come. It will take place after the thousand years are over. See Revelation 20:7-9. At that point, the earth will have been reduced to ruins by the events surrounding Jesus' second coming. Cities are broken down; men's factories and vineyards are turned into wilderness.

Later on (in the chapter titled, "A Thousand Years of What?") we will discuss in detail what takes place on earth during the millennium. For our purposes now, we need to see that no support exists in the Scriptures for the idea that life on earth will continue for seven more years after Christ comes and "raptures" His people secretly to heaven, or for the concept that Christ will reign *on earth* over all the nations for a thousand years.

Summing up, the texts cited in this chapter demonstrate these points: (a) that everyone on earth will see Christ when He comes; (b) that His return will not be a silent event; (c) that people on earth will not have a seven-year period of probation in which they have a second chance to get ready to meet the Lord; and (d) when Christ does come, the wicked alive at that time will be slain "with the brightness of his coming."

In our next chapter we will answer the question, What part will the Jews play in the final events on planet Earth? Is there a list of events related to modern Israel that must occur before the end can come and Christ return?

On the next two pages you will find a quick summary of New Testament teaching regarding Christ's second coming. The reader will find this two-page chart to be helpful in locating those texts which teach specific aspects of this coming event. After completing this book, these two pages will become even more meaningful.

Promises of His Return	Signs of His Return	A Literal Visible Event	Christ Descends From Heav
MATTHEW			
Matt. 16:27		Matt. 24:27, 30	
Matt. 26:63, 64	Matt. 24:3-31, 37-39	Matt. 25:31	
		Matt. 26:63, 64	
MARK			
		Mark 13:26	
Mark 13:26, 29-30	Mark 13:24-30	Mark 14:61, 62	
LUKE			
Luke 21:27, 28	Luke 13:8, 10, 24-26		
Acts 1:9-11	Luke 17:8-11, 26-30	Luke 21:27	Acts 1:9-1
Acts 3:20, 21	Luke 21:25-28	Acts 1:9-11	
JOHN			
John 14:1-3			
John 21:22		John 14:1-3	
1 John 2:28		1 John 3:2	Rev. 14:14
Rev. 1:7	Rev. 6:12-17	Rev.1:7	Rev. 19:11 21
Rev. 3:11	Rev. 13:16-18	Rev. 6:15-17	
Rev. 14:14		Rev. 19:11-16	
Rev. 22:7, 12, 20			
PAUL			
1 Cor. 1:7,8		Col. 3:4	
Phil. 3:20; 4:5	2 Thess. 2:3	1 Thess. 4:16	Phil. 3:20,
1 Tim. 6:14	1 Tim. 4:1-3	2 Thess. 1:7	1 Thess. 1:10
2 Tim. 4:8	2 Tim. 3:1-5	2 Tim. 4:7, 8	1 Thess. 4:16, 17
Titus 2:13		Titus 2:13	2 Thess. 1
Heb. 9:28		Heb. 9:28	
JAMES			
James 5:7, 8			
PETER			
1 Peter 1:7			
1 Peter 4:7	2 Peter 3:3, 4	1 Peter 1:7	
2 Peter 3:3-12		2 Peter 1:16	
JUDE			
	Jude 18		

the New Testament

Will Return with Power and Glory	Righteous Living & Dead to Meet Him	Rewards Given to Righteous and Wicked	Time of Coming Unknown
Matt. 13:40-43 Matt. 16:27 Matt. 24:30, 31	Matt. 24:30, 31	Matt. 13:30, 39-43 Matt. 13:47-50 Matt. 16:27	Matt. 24:36, 42-51
Matt. 25:31 Matt. 26:64	Matt. 25:31-34	Matt. 25:29, 30 Matt. 25:31-51	Matt. 25:13
Mark 8:38 Mark 13:26, 27 Mark 14:61, 62	Mark 13:26, 27	Mark 8:38	Mark 13:32-37
Luke 21:27	Luke 12:26-37 Luke 17:34-36	Luke 17:26-30 Luke 14:14	Luke 12:39, 40, 46 Luke 21:34-36
Rev. 1:7 Rev. 19:11-16	John 5:25, 28, 29 John 14:2, 3 1 John 3:2	John 5:28, 29 John 14:1-3 1 John 3:2, 3 Rev. 1:7 Rev. 6:13-17 Rev. 14:14-20 Rev. 19:11-21 Rev. 22:12	Rev. 3:3 Rev. 16:15
Cor. 15:51-54 Thess. 4:16, 17 Thess. 1:7 tus 2:13	1 Cor. 15:51-53 1 Thess. 4:16, 17	Rom. 2:6-8 1 Cor. 4:5 Col. 3:4 1 Thess. 4:16, 17 2 Thess. 1:8, 9 2 Tim. 4:1, 8 Heb. 9:28	1 Thess. 5:2
Peter 1:16		1 Peter 1:7 1 Peter 4:13; 5:4 2 Peter 3:10-13	2 Peter 3:10
Jude 14		Jude 14, 15	

Israel's Forfeited Future

In our previous chapter we discussed the rapture theory which teaches that the righteous will be secretly removed from planet Earth, leaving the rest of the world's inhabitants to carry on by themselves for another seven years, during which they will have a second chance for salvation.

Closely connected with that teaching are two others—that God will rely on the Jewish people during that seven-year interim to evangelize the wicked on earth and that modern Israel even prior to Christ's second coming will play a dominant political and evangelizing role during the last few years of earth's history.

In recent years many religious authors have made much of the establishment of the State of Israel in 1948, the famous Six-Day War of 1967, the occupation of the West Bank, and the capture of the ancient city of Jerusalem, explaining these events as direct fulfillments of Bible prophecy and ominous warnings of the nearness of the end.

Certain of these authors go on to describe authoritative scenarios revealing the parts that the authors expect Israel, Russia, China, and the United States to play in earth's final events.

Here are some typical statements:

"The Russians will make both an amphibious and

land invasion of Israel."—*The Late Great Planet Earth*, p. 146.

"China and possibly the U.S. and their allies will wipe out the Soviet army." "The Russian army will be destroyed in the Middle East, and their homeland will become 'a lake of fire.' "—*Countdown to Armageddon*, p. 90.

"The Oriental people, led by China, will battle the western nations in the planet's last great war."—*Countdown to Armageddon*, p. 95.

No doubt these accounts portray the author's conjectures, but are they what Scripture teaches?

First let's look at the basic theory that says that the Jews will play a key role as evangelizers of the end-time world and that the temple in Jerusalem will be rebuilt on the very spot where Solomon's Temple once stood. Both of these popular predictions rest on the premise that *all* prophecies given in the Old Testament about Abraham and his posterity must be literally fulfilled before the end can come.

With this in mind let's glance at a few of the predictions regarding God's original, ideal plan for Abraham and his seed.

God's Ideal Plan for Israel

●That the Israelites would inherit the land of Canaan "for ever." Genesis 13:14, 15.

●That Israel was to "blossom and bud, and fill the face of the world with fruit." Isaiah 27:6.

●That Jerusalem would become God's throne and all nations would "be gathered unto it." Jeremiah 3:17.

●That the temple in Jerusalem would "be called an house of prayer for all people." Isaiah 56:7.

●That "all the nations of the earth, which shall hear all the good that I do unto them . . . shall fear and tremble" before them (Jeremiah 33:9) and be afraid of them (Deuteronomy 28:10).

●That any nation which refused to serve Israel would be turned into a wasteland. See Isaiah 60:12.

God also predicted that the Israelites themselves would possess unparalleled prosperity (Deuteronomy 4:6-9; 7:12-15; 28:1-14), holiness of character (Leviticus 19:2), superior health (Exodus 15:26; Deuteronomy 7:13, 15), superior intellect (Deuteronomy 4:6), superior craftsmanship (Exodus 31:2-6; 35:33, 35), skill in agriculture and animal husbandry (Isaiah 51:3; Deuteronomy 7:13; 28:2-8; Malachi 3:8-11), and international fame (Deuteronomy 4:6-8; 7:6, 14; Jeremiah 33:9; Malachi 3:12).

If one could assume that all of the prophecies given in the Old Testament regarding Israel must be literally fulfilled before the Messiah returns, it would be fairly easy to catalog the various predictions, determine their probable order, and develop a chronological timetable for the end of the world. When we review certain end-time religious books on the market, we find indications that their authors have tried to do this very thing.

There is, however, a serious problem to this interpretation of Old Testament prophecies relating to Israel's future role in history: Prophecy is conditional. Virtually all of the predictions given to ancient Israel were conditional upon the people's obedience to God and faithfulness in following His ways.

Conditional Aspect of Prophecy

Prophetic utterances which demand specific human responses must never be viewed as absolute predictions. Such prophecies are conditional; if the people fail to meet the conditions, the prophecy cannot be fulfilled.

True, wonderful predictions of great power and prosperity were made to Israel regarding the Land of Palestine and the role God wanted them to play among the nations of the world. But repeatedly, in making these promises to the Israelites, God conditioned the results upon obedience. Time and again through various prophets God cautioned the Israelites that disobedience or apostasy would cancel the promised blessings. He warned repeatedly that the assurances of future prosperity and greatness could be forfeited.

This conditional aspect of prophecy can be easily seen in Deuteronomy 28, one of the great promise chapters of the Old Testament. The first fourteen verses guarantee a fabulous future for the Jewish people if they follow God's counsels and commandments. But the last fifty-four verses guarantee an equally bleak and dismal future for them if they refuse to follow God's counsels and commandments.

Israel's future was to be one of prosperity and international greatness if they obeyed, or one of decline and relative insignificance if they disobeyed. No less than half a dozen times in chapter 28 does God warn that the glorious future He planned for them depended totally upon their actions and responses.

Look at some of the warnings: "It shall come to pass, *if thou shalt hearken diligently unto the voice of the Lord thy God, to observe and to do all his commandments which I command thee this day*, that the Lord thy God will set thee on high above all nations of the earth." Verse 1, emphasis supplied.

"All these blessings shall come on thee, and overtake thee, *if thou shalt hearken unto the voice of the Lord*." Verse 2, emphasis supplied. See also verses 9, 13, 15, and 58.

Jeremiah declared the conditional nature of God's

promises to Israel when he said: "At what instant I shall speak concerning a nation, and concerning a kingdom, to build and to plant it; if it do evil in my sight, that it obey not my voice, then I will repent of the good, wherewith I said I would benefit them." Jeremiah 18:9, 10.

God's statement given to Nineveh through the prophet Jonah is a perfect example of this basic principle of conditional prophecy: "Yet forty days, and Nineveh shall be overthrown." Jonah 3:4. Although no condition was stated in the dire prediction, the fact that when the people of Nineveh repented God spared the city proves that the condition was there nonetheless. A superficial reading might conclude that God broke His own promise about the future of that nation. But the context assures us that the population's repentance turned the tide of destruction.

Other scriptural examples could be cited to support this important principle of interpretation of Bible prophecy. From what the Scriptures themselves declare, no promise of reward or prosperity will be fulfilled upon a disobedient and rebellious people.

You see, God will not violate the freedom of choice with which He has endowed the human race. If any particular group of people given opportunity for great blessings chooses to flaunt the conditions upon which those blessings have been offered, God respects the negative response and withdraws the offer.

The Messiah came, but "his own people received him not" (John 1:11, RSV), and Jesus had to abandon Israel to its self-chosen fate. Hence, we see Jesus just three days prior to His crucifixion lamenting over Jerusalem: "How often would I have gathered thy children together, even as a hen gathereth her chickens under her wings, *and ye would not!* Behold, your house is left unto you desolate." Matthew 23:37, 38, emphasis sup-plied.

Another reason why Christians today should not place any eschatological significance upon what has happened in the Middle East in the past forty years in-volves one of the most important teachings of the New Testament—that when ancient Israel rebelled against the conditions laid down for God's promised blessings, refused to share God's plan of salvation with the rest of the world, and finally rejected the Messiah Himself, God withdrew His special blessings from them and transferred the blessings to another group—spiritual Israel, which is the Christian church.

A New Israel Selected

Christ Himself declared this fact to the Jews of His day when He said, "The kingdom of God shall be taken from you, and given to a nation bringing forth the fruits thereof." Matthew 21:43.

He further illustrated this transfer of responsibility from the Jews to another group through the parable of the wicked husbandmen: "Then began he to speak to the people this parable; A certain man planted a vine-yard, and let it forth to husbandmen, and went into a far country for a long time. And at the season he sent a servant to the husbandmen, that they should give him of the fruit of the vineyard: but the husbandmen beat him, and sent him away empty. . . . Then said the lord of the vineyard, What shall I do? I will send my be-loved son: it may be they will reverence him when they see him. But when the husbandmen saw him, they . . . cast him out of the vineyard, and killed him. What therefore shall the lord of the vineyard do unto them? He shall come and destroy these husbandmen, and shall give the vineyard to others." Luke 20:9-16.

Did the Jewish leaders understand the messsage of the parable? They certainly did! Luke records, "When they heard it, they said, God forbid. . . . And the chief priests and the scribes the same hour sought to lay hands on him; . . . *for they perceived that he had spoken this parable against them.*" Verses 16-19, emphasis supplied.

Hearing Christ's parable about the vineyard, the Jewish leaders no doubt recalled the similar words of Isaiah and Jeremiah:

"And now, O inhabitants of Jerusalem, and men of Judah, judge, I pray you, betwixt me and my vineyard. What could have been done more to my vineyard, that I have not done in it? wherefore, when I looked that it should bring forth grapes, brought it forth wild grapes? And now go to; I will tell you what I will do to my vineyard: I will take away the hedge thereof, and it shall be eaten up; and break down the wall thereof, and it shall be trodden down: and I will lay it waste: it shall not be pruned, nor digged; but there shall come up briers and thorns: I will also command the clouds that they rain no rain upon it. *For the vineyard of the Lord of hosts is the house of Israel.*" Isaiah 5:3-7, emphasis supplied.

"*I had planted thee a noble vine*, wholly a right seed: how then art thou turned into the degenerate plant of a strange vine unto me?" Jeremiah 2:21, emphasis supplied.

Employing the same symbolism, Hosea predicted, "Israel is an empty vine." "*My God will cast them away*, because they did not hearken unto him: and they shall be wanderers among the nations." Hosea 10:1; 9:17, emphasis supplied.

Few things that Christ might have said could have upset the Jewish leaders quicker than to tell them that because of their unfruitfulness, God would replace the

Israelite vine with another vine not of the genetic lineage of Abraham.

Paul, writing to the church at Rome, confirmed the transfer of the kingdom of God to spiritual Israel when he declared, "God did not spare the natural branches"; "because of unbelief they were broken off"; "if some of the branches were broken off, and you, being a wild olive tree, were grafted in . . . do not boast against the branches." Romans 11:21, 20, 17, 18, NKJV.

Based on the New Testament, it is a mistake to expect the Old Testament prophecies to be fulfilled on the basis of blood descent from Abraham, Isaac, and Jacob—whether we call those descendants Jews or Israelites.

It is no longer natural birth that interests God, but rebirth. The true Jew is not one of the flesh, but one of the spirit. See Romans 2:28, 29.

"There is neither Jew nor Greek, there is neither bond nor free, there is neither male nor female: for ye are all one in Christ Jesus. And if ye be Christ's then are ye Abraham's seed, and heirs according to the promise." Galatians 3:28, 29; see also Romans 9:6-8.

However, in proclaiming this transition of responsibilities, God did not leave out individual Jews who should wish to remain part of His true vine. Paul wrote in Romans 11 about Jews who believed in Christ, assuring them that they were grafted back into the vine. See verses 23, 24.

Yet the emphasis in the New Testament is that it is the Christians, not the Israelites, who now occupy the special status of God's agents and representatives. They are now "God's own people" commissioned to the world. 1 Peter 2:9, 10. To Christ's followers, not to the nation of Israel, God gave the charge, "Make disciples of all nations." Matthew 28:19, RSV. To teach that the nation of Israel has this task yet to accomplish in order to carry out this commission is to reject an important message of the New Testament.

Moreover, such a teaching simply doesn't fit into the chronology that Jesus Himself laid down. According to Jesus, "This gospel of the kingdom shall be preached in all the world for a witness unto all nations; and *then* shall the end come." Matthew 24:14, emphasis supplied. Since we know from the same gospel that the Christians will be the ones specifically responsible for this task (see Matthew 28:19, 20), what remains for the Jews to do? After the completion of the gospel commission, there will be no further need for special agents or witnesses.

Consequently, considering the conditional nature of God's Old Testament prophecies to ancient Israel and the fact that the New Testament has placed the work and responsibilities of ancient Israel upon the Christian church, it seems scripturally clear that the Jews as a nation have no special part in God's last-day activities—either during the time immediately preceding the millennium or during the millennium itself.

Nowhere in the New Testament do we find support for the belief that the temple in Jerusalem must be rebuilt before the Messiah returns. Nowhere do we find a New Testament passage that says the Jews will become God's evangelists during end time. Nowhere in the New Testament do we find proof that the literal nation of Israel will become the focus of the world's interest and attention. Such teachings cannot be supported by the New Testament.

In our next chapter we will look at 15 true signs of Christ's near return, ten of which Christ Himself gave us.

When Will the End Come?

On Sunday, May 18, 1980, following two months of incessant warnings—earth tremors, ash geysers, and steam clouds from the expanding crater at its top—Washington state's famous Mount St. Helens exploded.

Statistics published about the 8:32 a.m. blast almost boggle the mind: the explosion had the impact of 50 million tons of TNT and was as destructive as the largest hydrogen bomb ever built (a 50-megaton bomb); it exceeded by 2500 times the atomic blast that leveled Hiroshima during World War II; it turned 156 square miles of scenic wilderness into a landscape as desolate as the moon; it leveled 2 billion board feet of virgin forest (enough lumber to construct 200,000 five-room, all-wood homes); it killed thirty-two people and left another sixty missing; and it blew into the atmosphere, according to one TV newscaster, the equivalent of one ton of volcanic dust for every man, woman, and child living on the face of the earth.

"The moon looks like a golf course compared to what's up there," former President Carter exclaimed after returning from a helicopter survey of the devastation five days later.

After calling the destruction "the worst thing I have ever seen" and "literally indescribable," he predicted that within a year the peak and its devastated surroundings could become "a tourist attraction that will equal the Grand Canyon."

Aside from the many obvious lessons this volcanic explosion can teach twentieth-century humans (from the insignificance of mortal beings to the awesomeness of the planet on which we ride through space), two specific lessons should apply to all of us. The first involves the gullibility of the human species; the second concerns the unwillingness of many humans to heed clear warnings of impending doom.

We Are Too Gullible

It seems that most humans—whether on the battlefield or in a boat without a life jacket—refuse to believe that disaster *can* happen to us. We are too gullible. We always like to think that it's the other guy who will die in a car wreck; that it's someone else's home that will be burglarized; that only other people who smoke cigarettes will die of lung cancer. We refuse to visualize ourselves in such unacceptable situations.

Obviously, such was the case with the scores of sightseers, vacationers, and sportsmen who flocked to Mount St. Helens that fateful May weekend. Had they really believed the mountain could explode on them and kill them or that they likely would not have time to escape to safety, would they have ventured so near the ticking geological time bomb?

The second lesson we should derive from this awesome demonstration of earth's unharnessed power involves our general unwillingness to heed warnings of even cataclysmic events.

Such was the case when hurricane Camille struck the Mississippi and Louisiana coastline in 1969 and killed more than 300 people—nearly all of whom had ignored frequent warnings of the oncoming disaster. Such was also the case with the Mount St. Helens explosion.

For nearly two months—from March 20 through May 17—Mount St. Helens had belched steam, smoke, and ash and had shaken with dozens of tremors and earthquakes. It had sent out small rivers of ash, which froze on its sides. Small avalanches had cascaded down its slopes. Within three weeks a 1700-foot-wide crater had opened a gaping mouth at the top of the peak, and the north side of the mountain (where the blast was later to occur) had bulged outward at the rate of four to six feet a day.

In spite of all these obvious signs that internal pressure was building up, hundreds flocked to the mountain to sight-see, to fish, and to camp. They tore down or drove around roadblocks intended to keep them out. They ignored the advice of experts.

One resident—84-year-old Harry Truman, owner of the Mount St. Helens Lodge—refused every attempt to evacuate him from his beloved home at the north base of the mountain. "There's nothing that mountain could do to scare me off," said Truman, who had been living on the mountain for fifty-four years. "No one knows more about this mountain than Harry," he added, "and it don't dare blow up on him."

They Gambled Their Lives

Today Harry and his famous lodge lie under dozens of feet of volcanic mud. He, along with nearly a hundred others, gambled their lives with the mountain—and lost.

Why is it that we humans are so unwilling to heed obvious warnings of impending calamities that could spell our doom? And if this be true of volcanoes and hurricanes, isn't it even more true regarding the future of this whole earth?

As the Mount St. Helens explosion was preceded by numerous warnings over a period of time, so the second coming of Christ will be preceded by signs, or warnings, pointing toward the climactic event.

Ten Specific Events

Christ Himself gave us at least ten specific events or conditions that would take place prior to His return and which would serve as warnings of earth's final days. Let's look at these and compare them with the days in which we live. We may be surprised to see how many have already been fulfilled.

The three chapters recording Christ's words about the final days of earth's history are Matthew 24, Mark 13, and Luke 21. In these chapters, Christ answers two questions put to Him by His disciples: "Tell us, when shall these things be [the destruction of Jerusalem—see verses 1 and 2]? and what shall be the sign of thy coming, and of the end of the world?" Matthew 24:3.

Eliminating the passages that refer exclusively to the Roman destruction of Jerusalem—an event that took place in 70 A.D.—we here chart the ten signs given by Christ as signs of His coming and the end of the world:

Sign of Christ's Return	Matthew 24	Mark 13	Luke 21
Wars among many nations	verse 7	verse 8	verses 9, 10
Famines and earthquakes	verse 7	verse 8	verse 11
Iniquity as in Noah's days	verses 12, 37		
Gospel to whole world	verse 14	verse 10	

Period of great tribulation	verse 21	verse 24	
False christs and prophets	verses 23, 24	verse 22	verse 8
Sun darkened	verse 29	verse 24	verse 25
Moon darkened	verse 29	verse 24	verse 25
Stars fall from heaven	verse 29	verse 25	verse 25
Powers of heaven shaken	verse 29	verse 25	verse 26

To these ten signs given by Christ we can add five more recorded by other Bible writers: a dramatic increase in knowledge (see Daniel 12:4); an increase in demonic activity (see Revelation 16:13, 14); an increase in lawlessness (see 2 Timothy 3:2-4); a departure from scriptural faith (see 2 Timothy 4:3, 4); and a widening gap between the rich and the poor, with class struggles and revolutions (see James 5:1-8).

Now let's examine these fifteen signs to see how many of them already have been or are presently being fulfilled.

1. *A period of tribulation.*

"Then there shall be great tribulation, such as was not since the beginning of the world to this time." Matthew 24:21.

According to Christ, the long period of tribulation would occur between the destruction of Jerusalem (70 A.D.) and the end of the world. While it is true that a number of short periods of persecution befell the church over the early centuries—first from the Jewish leaders (see Acts 4:1-3), then the Gentiles (see Acts 16:19-24), and finally the Romans—the longest period of religious suppression of conscience stretched from 538 A.D. to 1798 A.D. under the Roman church.

Tens of thousands of Christians who dared to believe differently from the authorized dogma were persecuted, exiled, imprisoned, tortured and executed.*

Eventually the Protestant Reformation, the French enlightenment, the American Bill of Rights, and the capture and imprisonment of the pope in 1798 marked the end of this 1260-year-long period of tribulation.† See Revelation 11:2, 3; Daniel 7:25; 8:14; Revelation 12:13-16; 13:5-7. This progression of events takes us down near the final period of history known as "the last days."

2. *The sun shall be darkened.*

"But in those days, after that tribulation, the sun shall be darkened." Mark 13:24.

Paraphrasing a familiar Old Testament passage (Joel 2:30, 31), Christ issued another specific sign that would point out the beginning of the final period of earth's history.

Historical records clearly identify May 19, 1780, as the Great Dark Day of North America, when beginning at about 9:00 a.m. daylight turned into darkness over a vast portion of populated United States, and the following night the moon appeared as blood. (Many encyclopedias contain references to this unique event, which witnesses at the time viewed as a sign from the Lord regarding the end of the world. Its timeliness, oc-

---

*For more information, see *Encyclopaedia Britannica* for entries under "Inquisition"—"Medieval Inquisition," "Spanish Inquisition," and "Roman Inquisition."

†Although the 1260-year tribulation period extends to 1798, the actual persecution ended around 1755. Jesus had said the persecution would be "shortened." Matthew 24:22. Then He said that the sun would be darkened within the prophesied tribulation period but after the persecution had stopped. This means we must look for the dark day after 1755 and before 1798. As it turned out, the sun was darkened in 1780. Right on time!

curring as the religious-tribulation period was concluding, adds more authenticity to its validity.)

3. *The moon won't shed light.*

"But in those days . . . the moon shall not give her light." Mark 13:24.

On the night of May 19, 1780, following the Dark Day, residents of New England witnessed the rise of an eerie, blood-red moon. (Obviously, the earlier event could not have resulted from an eclipse of the sun, for the darkened moon that evening was nearly at full-moon stage.)

4. *The stars shall fall.*

"And the stars shall fall from heaven." Matthew 24:29. "The stars of heaven fell unto the earth, even as a fig tree casteth her untimely figs, when she is shaken of a mighty wind." Revelation 6:13.

Just thirty-five years after the close of the 1260-year tribulation period that Christ warned about, another striking event occurred. Concerning the meteoric shower of November 12-13, 1833, Professor Dennison Almsted, of Yale University, wrote, "To form some idea of the phenomenon, the reader may imagine a constant succession of fireballs, resembling rockets, radiating in all directions from a point in the heavens. . . . [There were] meteors of various sizes and degrees of splendor: some were mere points but others were larger than Jupiter or Venus."—*Silliman Journal*, 25:354-411 and 26:132-174. Quoted in Charles P. Olivier, *Meteors* (Baltimore: Williams and Wilkins Co., 1925), p. 24.

Dr. Humphreys, president of St. Johns College, Annapolis, Maryland, adds, "During the period just previous to the dawn, it was observed by many intelligent persons in the city, whose statements coincide most perfectly, as to the almost infinite number of the meteors. In the words of most, they fell like flakes of snow."—Humphreys, *American Journal of Science*, 25:372. Quoted by Everett Dick in "The Falling of the Stars," *The Advent Review and Sabbath Herald*, November 2, 1933, p. 11.

According to available records, this event rates as one of the greatest displays of celestial fireworks seen by mankind since the creation of the world. Significantly, the falling stars (or meteors) followed within a few years of the darkening of the sun and moon mentioned by Christ as indicators of the beginning of earth's final period of history.

5. *Wars will occur among many nations.*

"Ye shall hear of wars and rumours of wars. . . . For nation shall rise against nation, and kingdom against kingdom." Matthew 24:6, 7.

According to Christ, earth's end-time period would be highlighted by major wars involving many nations. It should come as no surprise to us living today that only in this century has the earth witnessed two world wars of such magnitude that they made all previous wars seem like minor skirmishes.

Moreover, only in the past twenty or thirty years has man possessed sufficient destructive power literally at his fingertips to obliterate all life from this planet in a matter of a few hours.

This destructive force is, in the words of Dr. Carl Sagan, "enough to obliterate a million Hiroshimas. But there are fewer than 3000 cities on the Earth with populations of 100,000 or more. You cannot find anything like a million Hiroshimas to obliterate. . . . Thus, there are vastly more nuclear weapons than are needed for any plausible deterrence of a potential adversary."—*Parade*, October 30, 1983.

Yet as you read these words, ten new countries presently have the capability to build nuclear weapons (Argentina, Canada, West Germany, Israel, Italy, Japan, Pakistan, South Africa, Sweden, and Switzerland), and eleven more could have nuclear bombs by 1989 (Australia, Austria, Belgium, Brazil, Denmark, Iraq, South Korea, Netherlands, Norway, Spain, and Taiwan).—*Newsweek*, December 5, 1983.

Because of these sobering facts, the authoritative Stockholm International Peace Research Institute (comprised of 200 experts from 25 countries) warned not long ago that as more nations develop nuclear weaponry, "stable nuclear deterrence as we have known it will become impossible and war will become inevitable."

Regarding this final period of history, Jesus said, "Men's hearts [will be] failing them for fear, and for looking after those things which are coming on the earth." Luke 21:26. How well His words fit our world today!

In our next chapter we will examine the remaining ten signs that show we are living in the final days of earth's history and that the end is "near, even at the doors."

Time Is Running Out

In the preceding chapter we noted how humans generally ignore warnings that a disaster is near, believing instead that no calamity can possibly strike them. Like lemmings, we run with the pack, never asking where we are headed until it's too late to stop. We also discussed five specific signs that Christ gave to point out the final period of earth's history: (1) a long period of persecution (tribulation), (2) the darkening of the sun, (3) the darkening of the moon, (4) the falling stars, and (5) wars among many nations.

Now let's look at the remaining ten signs that show us time is rapidly running out.

6. *An increase in earthquakes.*

"There will be great earthquakes in various places, and famines and pestilences." Luke 21:11, NKJV.

During the past 400 years, earthquakes per century have dramatically increased. In the sixteenth century, for example, we find records of only 253 earthquakes, in the eighteenth—640 quakes, and during the nineteenth century—2119 quakes.

But in the twentieth century, earthquakes have become so severe and so frequent that they have killed more than a million humans since World War II alone. And scientists predict that more major catastrophic quakes are inevitable. "When the *big* quake does hit—as it surely will in California if not Seattle or Salt Lake

City or Charleston or even New England—the devastation will be unimaginable."—*U.S. News and World Report*, November 14, 1983.

Obviously planet Earth is waxing "old like a garment." Isaiah 51:6.

But note that in addition to earthquakes, Jesus warned that "famines, and pestilences" would increase near the end of time.

Famines occur when available food supply can no longer meet the demand, when there are too many mouths for the available food.

Significantly, never before in earth's history have we witnessed such a population explosion as we have today—*with the world gaining in two years' time as*

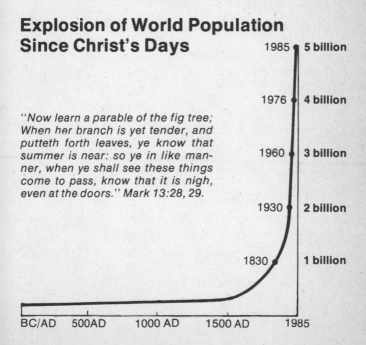

Explosion of World Population Since Christ's Days

1985 • 5 billion

1976 • 4 billion

"Now learn a parable of the fig tree; When her branch is yet tender, and putteth forth leaves, ye know that summer is near: so ye in like manner, when ye shall see these things come to pass, know that it is nigh, even at the doors." Mark 13:28, 29.

1960 • 3 billion

1930 • 2 billion

1830 • 1 billion

BC/AD   500AD   1000 AD   1500 AD   1985

many humans as were alive on earth when Christ spoke those words!

While it took all of human history to reach a worldwide population of one billion humans by 1830, it required only one hundred years to add a second billion (1930), thirty years for the third billion (1960), and sixteen years for the fourth billion (1976).—*Reader's Digest 1979 Almanac*, p. 193. At the present rate of growth (see chart), world population will hit seven billion by the year 2000 and nine billion by 2010—just twenty-five years from now.

If we think the world has famines now, what must the next ten or twenty years hold in store as world population grows by quantum leaps and bounds?

7. *Earth will be as it was in Noah's days.*

"As the days of Noe were, so shall also the coming of the Son of man be. For as in the days that were before the flood they were eating and drinking, marrying and giving in marriage . . . ; so shall also the coming of the Son of man be." Matthew 24:37-39.

"The love of many shall wax cold." Matthew 24:12.

Even as recently as fifty years ago, few sociologists foresaw the dramatic deterioration of the family that we have witnessed in our lifetime. Current statistics reveal a society almost without love:

• *15 percent* of all families in the U.S. report that a spouse has been married more than once.

• *22 percent* of U.S. households in 1980 were comprised of a single person living alone. (In 1940 single-person households numbered only 7 percent.)

• *30 percent* of all U.S. pregnancies end in abortion (with more than 1.5 million abortions every year).

• *The divorce rate* in the past eighty years has skyrocketed from eight percent in 1900 to *50 percent* in the 1980s (see chart on p. 79). While these statistics

Leap in U.S. Divorce Rates

"The love of many shall wax cold."
Matthew 24:12

The dramatic increase in U.S. divorce rates (expressed as a ratio of divorces per marriages during the years indicated) illustrates the uniqueness of the days in which we live.

represent only the United States, many countries of the world are experiencing similar problems.

8. *A dramatic increase in knowledge.*

"Daniel, shut up the words, and seal the book, even to the time of the end: many shall run to and fro, and knowledge shall be increased." Daniel 12:4.

Although we could list pages of facts to show that knowledge has increased in our days as *never* before in the world's history, perhaps just two examples will suffice.

The first involves computers, which have already passed through five generations—vacuum tubes, transistors, simple integrated circuits, microchips, and now magnetic bubble memories and Josephson junctions. So rapidly has computer power and capability grown that problem-solving speed has doubled every two years since 1951.

For example, "the best computers in 1957 would have taken 30 years and $10 million in computing time to solve a problem involving two-dimensional airflow over an airplane wing. A Cray 1 [supercomputer] can solve it today in 15 to 30 minutes, at a cost of less than $1000."—*Science Digest*, September 1983.

And the newest and most powerful supercomputer in the world, the Cray 2 (which has a central processing unit 26 inches high and 38 inches long and sits in a small glass aquarium immersed in liquid fluorocarbon), can function at speeds *in excess of one billion operations per second!* (Its immediate predecessor, the Cray 1, was 9 feet long and could conduct only about 160 million operations per second.)

The second example centers around this shocking fact about human knowledge: the midway point for all human knowledge, according to research studies, *lies approximately eight years ago*. Or put another way, "By the time a child born today graduates from college the knowledge in the world will be four times as great. By the time that child is fifty years old, it will be thirty-two times as great and 97 percent of everything known in the world will have been learned since the time he was born."—H. L. Wilmington, *Signs of the Times* (Wheaton, Illinois: Tyndale House, 1982), p. 28.

What would Daniel say if he could witness the explosion of knowledge we see today? Knowledge certainly has been increased!

9. *An increased interest in spiritism.*

"I saw three unclean spirits like frogs come out of the mouth of the dragon, and out of the mouth of the beast, and out of the mouth of the false prophet. For they are the spirits of devils, working miracles, which go forth unto the kings of the earth." Revelation 16:13, 14.

One hardly needs to cite statistics to confirm the revived interest we see everywhere in the occult, psychic phenomena, ESP, black magic, astrology and parapsychology. Nearly every week one can read newspaper headlines in the nation's tabloids announcing supposed new evidence for life after death—stories about people "crossing over" into the spirit world and meeting relatives long since dead.

Yet the Bible tells us that communicating with the dead is impossible: "For the living know that they shall die: but the dead know not any thing. . . . Their love, and their hatred, and their envy, is now perished; neither have they any more a portion for ever in any thing that is done under the sun." Ecclesiastes 9:5, 6.

The Scriptures state that when a person dies "in that very day his thoughts perish." Psalm 146:4. He cannot communicate with the living or with anyone else (see Job 7:10), because he is asleep (see John 11:11-14) and will remain asleep in the grave until the resurrection (see John 11:43, 44; Job 14:12-14).

10. *An increase in lawlessness.*

"Know this, that in the last days perilous times will come: For men will be lovers of themselves, lovers of money, boasters, proud, blasphemers, disobedient to parents, unthankful, unholy, unloving, unforgiving, slanderers, without self-control, brutal, despisers of good, traitors, headstrong, haughty, lovers of pleasure rather than lovers of God." 2 Timothy 3:1-4, NKJV.

Toll of World Violence

Annual deaths caused by
international terrorism

*"In the last days perilous times will
come: For men will be . . . without self-
control, brutal, despisers of good."*
2 Timothy 3:1, 3, NKJV.

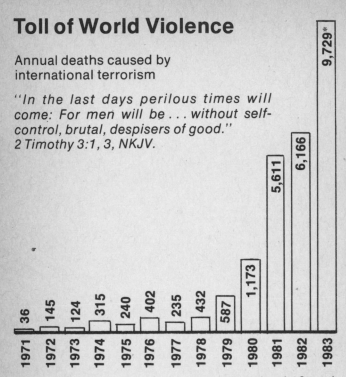

1971	36
1972	145
1973	124
1974	315
1975	240
1976	402
1977	235
1978	432
1979	587
1980	1,173
1981	5,611
1982	6,166
1983	9,729*

(*Estimate based on 1st 9 mos.)

A glance at a few daily newspapers or weekly news
magazines reveals the extent of lawlessness our soci-
ety today has achieved. The headlines reveal the con-
dition of planet Earth: "Youth Gangs Are Back" *(U.S.
News and World Report);* "A $40-Billion Crime Wave
Swamps American Business" *(U.S. News and World
Report);* "Catching a New Breed of Killer" *(Time);*
"The Youth Crime Plague" *(Time);* "Violent Crime
Found Pervasive in Nation" (The *Washington Post);*
"Violence in America—Getting Worse?" *(U.S. News
and World Report).*

Recent FBI statistics reveal that a violent crime is committed on an average of once every 25 seconds in the United States. Every 25 minutes someone is murdered; every 7 minutes some woman is forcibly raped; every minute 2 cars are stolen; every 59 seconds someone is robbed; every 48 seconds there is an aggravated assault, and every 9 seconds a home is burglarized.

Over the 20-year period of 1960 to 1980 the rate of violent crimes (murder, rape, robbery, aggravated assault) per 100,000 population in the United States rose 360 percent. Property crime (burglary, larceny, auto theft) increased 308 percent.

If these U.S. figures at all represent the rest of the world, then truly this generation is corrupt!

Another example of the lawlessness and brutality of our generation involves the mounting casualties from international terrorism. In a thirteen-year period deaths from international terrorism soared from 36 in 1971 to an estimated 9729 for 1983 (see chart).

11. *A departure from scriptural faith.*

"There will be false teachers among you, who will secretly bring in destructive heresies. . . . And many will follow their destructive ways, because of whom the way of truth will be blasphemed." 2 Peter 2:1, 2, NKJV.

"For the time will come when they will not endure sound doctrine; but after their own lusts shall they heap to themselves teachers, having itching ears; and they shall turn away their ears from the truth, and shall be turned unto fables." 2 Timothy 4:3, 4.

"Let no one deceive you by any means; for that Day will not come unless the falling away comes first, and the man of sin is revealed, . . . who . . . sits as God in the temple of God, showing himself that he is God." 2 Thessalonians 2:3, 4, NKJV.

The vast proliferation of denominations and churches that we see today—each with its own particular set of beliefs—certainly reveals the lack of consensus among Christians regarding the teachings of Scripture. No wonder Christians everywhere are asking, "Does God have a church on earth?"

12. *False Christs and false prophets shall arise*.

"False Christs and false prophets shall rise, and shall shew signs and wonders, to seduce, if it were possible, even the elect." Mark 13:22.

For brevity's sake, we cite only one instance—the story of Reverend Jim Jones, who led 914 followers to commit mass suicide in the jungles of Guyana—to illustrate that false prophets have made their appearance in our generation.

Such movements, dramatically on the increase, fulfill Christ's warning that in the last days "many false prophets shall rise, and shall deceive many." Matthew 24:11.

13. *Growing tension between haves and have-nots*.

James wrote that the end time would be characterized by serious clashes between rich and poor and between capital and labor.

"Go to now, ye rich men, weep and howl for your miseries that shall come upon you. . . . Ye have heaped treasure together for the last days." "The coming of the Lord draweth nigh." James 5:1-3, 8.

Increasing prevalence of strikes by laborers against management, attended often with ugly demonstrations should tell us something as we compare this relatively modern phenomenon with the apostle James's prediction. Add to these industrial class struggles agrarian uprisings against the oppressive rich in many developing nations and we see fulfillment of this prophecy taking on international dimensions.

14. *Gospel to the whole world.*

"This gospel of the kingdom shall be preached in all the world for a witness unto all nations; and then shall the end come." Matthew 24:14.

In spite of the sad state of world affairs that we have discussed in this and the preceding chapter, today as never before the gospel of Christ is reaching out to virtually every corner of the globe.

As in the days immediately prior to the fall of Jerusalem, when the apostle Paul declared that the gospel was even then being "preached to every creature which is under heaven" (Colossians 1:23), so now prior to the return of Jesus as Lord and King is the gospel being proclaimed—by radio, TV, the printed word, and in person—as "a witness unto all nations" (Matthew 24:14).

Today more than a billion of earth's inhabitants (or about one out of four) belong to one of Christianity's churches. Christian missionaries are all around the globe today, warning millions of the nearness of Christ's return. And in contrast to a world 200 years ago, when the printed Bible was available in only a handful of languages, today the Scriptures in whole or part have been translated into more than 1,500 different languages, making it the single most accessible book in human history.

Christ did not predict that the whole world would be converted to Christianity. He said, "The gospel must first be published among all nations." Mark 13:10. This is happening before our eyes—today!

15. *The powers of heaven will be shaken.*

"The powers that are in heaven shall be shaken. And then shall they see the Son of man coming in the clouds with great power and glory." Mark 13:25, 26.

The final sign—and by far the most spectacular—

will take place when Christ upsets all the powers of heaven and earth during His return to planet Earth.

Another passage describes the event in these words: "The heaven departed as a scroll when it is rolled together; and every mountain and island were moved out of their places." "For the great day of his wrath is come." Revelation 6:14, 17.

Interestingly, the two verses prior to this passage in Revelation (verses 12 and 13) refer to the darkening of the sun and moon and to the great meteor shower that Christ foretold, the "falling of the stars." For more than a hundred years, planet Earth has been circling between verses 13 and 14, waiting for Christ to announce, "He that is unjust, let him be unjust still: and he which is filthy, let him be filthy still: and he that is righteous, let him be righteous still: and he that is holy, let him be holy still. And, behold, I come quickly; and my reward is with me, to give every man according as his work shall be." Revelation 22:11, 12.

While it is true that no human on earth can know the day or hour of Christ's return, the fifteen signs given by the Scriptures clearly show "it is near, even at the doors." Matthew 24:33. It remains for us to be sure that we are ready at any time, so we can greet the soon-coming Saviour. And being ready isn't all that hard if we follow the simple directions as given in the Bible. In fact, Christ in His love for us has made it possible for everyone who believes in Him. See John 3:16. It involves only a willingness to submit to His instructions and open the life in faith to His abiding presence. And when you know how gracious He is, who wouldn't want to do that and experience the miracle of His transforming grace? That's the everlasting gospel, or the good news of salvation, in a nutshell.

God's Three Final Warnings

In the last two chapters we discovered fifteen clear, specific signs showing that time has nearly run out for planet Earth.

So precarious has the situation become in recent months that on December 22, 1983, the 47 scientists who monitor the Doomsday Clock* of the *Bulletin of the Atomic Scientists* moved the clock forward one more minute—to three minutes before midnight—the closest the clock has stood in thirty years to what scientists believe is the end of the world via a nuclear holocaust.—*Time*, January 2, 1984.

Truly we are living in the final days of earth's history—with very little time remaining to prepare for Christ's return.

With this thought in mind, one wonders just what kind of final warning or warnings God has planned for this concluding period of history.

---

*"The Doomsday Clock" was invented in 1947 by a group of nuclear scientists to depict graphically how near they feel the world is to a nuclear war. Originally set at seven minutes to midnight, the clock has shifted 11 times in 36 years, the most recent changes being these: 1972—11:48 (SALT began); 1974—11:51 (SALT stalled); 1980—11:53 (nations become irrational); 1981—11:56 (nuclear war considered possible); and 1983—11:57 (national leaders act as if ready to use nuclear weapons).

Interestingly, one chapter in Revelation describes in some detail three specific proclamations, or warnings, that must go to the world before the earth can be harvested. In the rich symbolism of Revelation, they are described as the messages of three flying angels. Let's look at them:

Angels Flying With Messages

"I saw another angel fly in the midst of heaven, having the everlasting gospel to preach unto them that dwell on the earth, and to every nation, and kindred, and tongue, and people, saying with a loud voice, Fear God, and give glory to him; for the hour of his judgment is come: and worship him that made heaven, and earth, and the sea, and the fountains of waters. And there followed another angel, saying, Babylon is fallen, is fallen, that great city, because she made all nations drink of the wine of the wrath of her fornication. And the third angel followed them, saying with a loud voice, If any man worship the beast and his image, and receive his mark in his forehead, or in his hand, the same shall drink of the wine of the wrath of God, which is poured out without mixture into the cup of his indignation." Revelation 14:6-10.

We know that these three angels' messages are the final warnings to planet Earth because the very next event John witnessed after seeing these three angels and hearing their warnings was "a white cloud, and upon the cloud one sat like unto the Son of man, having on his head a golden crown, and in his hand a sharp sickle. And another angel came out of the temple, crying with a loud voice to him that sat on the cloud, Thrust in thy sickle, and reap: for the time is come for thee to reap; for the harvest of the earth is ripe. And he that sat on the cloud thrust in his sickle on the earth; and the earth was reaped." Revelation 14:14-16.

Perhaps the first question we might like to ask about these three angels with messages for earth's final inhabitants is, Does God really plan to use angels to warn the earth of its end?

Nowhere in Scripture do we find evidence that angels have been commissioned with the responsibility of preaching the gospel or of announcing Heaven's warning of earth's end. Christ gave that task to His followers (see Matthew 28:18-20), not to literal angels flying through the sky. It is true, of course, that angels *assist* humans in the work of proclaiming the gospel (see Hebrews 1:14), but that is not the primary emphasis in this passage.

As with the other symbols in Revelation, these angels represent or symbolize something else—in this case witnessing Christians living at the end of time.

Therefore, these three heavenly "messengers," one following another, each with a new emphasis to add to the preceeding message, represent a religious movement of Christians with a unique threefold message for earth's inhabitants at the end of time.

Now let's look briefly at the three final warnings to be proclaimed as planet Earth spins toward its encounter with eternity. As we examine the messages, let's also ask ourselves whether any religious movement today is preaching them.

The First Angel's Message

"Fear God, and give glory to him; for the hour of his judgment is come: and worship him that made heaven, and earth, and the sea, and the fountains of waters." Revelation 14:7.

This first message includes the preaching of "the everlasting gospel'' (verse 6), coupled with a warning that judgment time for earth has arrived (verse 7). It also includes a strong appeal for earth's inhabitants to return again to worshiping (and believing in) a Creator-God.

Never before in human history has the message of a Creator-God been more relevant than during the last 130 years. Before 1860 virtually all Christians everywhere believed that God created the world as the Bible says He did. But since Darwin published his book on evolution in 1859, belief in God as Creator has dwindled and the theory of evolution has largely replaced it, both in the public schools and the scientific community.

God's first warning for this doomed planet challenges us *not* to accept evolution, but to return to worshiping the God who *created* this world and all life on it. As we look around, therefore, in these last days to locate a religious movement proclaiming God's final warnings, we should look for a group who teaches (a) the everlasting gospel of salvation through Christ, (b) that "the hour of his judgment is come," and (c) that by creation, not through evolution, is how humans arrived on earth.

Significantly, thinking especially of this final point, God originally gave mankind a weekly reminder of His creative work, and He placed that reminder in the heart of His Ten Commandments by saying, "In six days the Lord made heaven and earth, the sea, and all that in them is, and rested the seventh day: wherefore the Lord blessed the Sabbath day, and hallowed it." Exodus 20:11. One cannot but wonder, if Christians had been keeping God's seventh-day Sabbath throughout the past 2000 years, would the theory of evolution have captured so much of the world's interest?

The Second Angel's Message

"Babylon is fallen, is fallen, that great city, because she made all nations drink of the wine of the wrath of her fornication." Revelation 14:8.

Obviously this message cannot be taken literally, for the ancient city of Babylon was in ruins even when John wrote, let alone at the end time. But there are so many references to "Babylon" in both Christian and Jewish literature of the first centuries of the Christian era that there can be no doubt that this cryptic use of the word represents Rome—either the city of Rome (as in 1 Peter 5:13) or the empire of Rome.

The Roman empire fell in A.D. 476—so if, as we believe, the second angel is giving his message at the present time, he is not using the term *Babylon* to refer to that ancient government. Is there some other world power, headquartered in Rome, that he may be talking about? It would have to be strong enough to force all nations to follow its example. (The angel says it "made all nations" do something.) It would have to be a religious power, because the angel says that what it made the nations do was "drink of the wine . . . of her fornication." Fornication in the Bible is sometimes the same kind of illicit sex we know about today, but when used as a symbol—as it is here—it refers to mixing—or adulterating—good religion with bad religion. And another thing. This power would have to have a history of great strength followed by a (recent) period of weakness, because the angel says it has fallen. From other passages in the Scriptures we believe the weakness would be followed by greater strength and popularity than ever before.

Does any organization or government fit all these criteria—a religious power (a church?) with enormous international influence that suddenly falls from power

in the recent past but will be seen to regain its power—
and with headquarters in Rome? Can it be anything
other than the Roman Catholic Church which once had
so much power it could forbid King Henry VIII to divorce his wife, but which became so weak in the recent
past that its leader was taken prisoner by a French
army (in 1798), but which is becoming immensely popular and powerful again under Pope John Paul II? If so,
then God recognizes many Roman Catholics as belong-
ing to Himself. He calls them "my people" and, when
Babylon falls He sends a special message from heaven
addressed particularly to them. It urges, "Come out of
her, *my people*." See Revelation 18:1-4.

This call to flee Babylon should not go unheeded as
we see rapidly fulfilling events transpire around us,
showing how near we are to the end of human history.
Now, let's examine the third and final warning for
earth's last generation.

The Third Angel's Message
*"If any man worship the beast and his image, and
receive his mark in his forehead, or in his hand, the
same shall drink of the wine of the wrath of God."*
Revelation 14:9, 10.

The Bible tells us that "God sent not his Son into the
world to condemn the world; but that the world
through him might be saved." John 3:17. How gracious and good God is! And how He longs to have everyone know of the salvation He has provided!

What was true of Christ's incarnation and life on
earth is also true of these three angels' messages. They
are being proclaimed here at the culmination of history, not to condemn or frighten, but to arouse humans
everywhere to the lateness of the hour and the seriousness of the issues we face—and, most of all, to entreat

us to accept Christ as our Saviour and Lord that we might be saved.

"Have I any desire, says the Lord God, for the death of a wicked man? Would I not rather that he should mend his ways and live?" Ezekiel 18:23, NEB.

The message of the third angel reveals the basic issues that will emerge in the final struggle over human hearts and souls. At the very end of time, Revelation declares, two classes of people will emerge: (1) those who "worship the beast and his image, and receive his mark" and (2) God's people—the true followers of Jesus Christ who accept the everlasting gospel and reject the mark of the beast.

According to Revelation 14, God's people at the end of time will be identifiable by two distinct attributes—*obedience* and *trust*. We see this plainly in verse 12: "Here is the patience of the saints: here are they that keep the commandments of God, and the faith of Jesus."

A parallel passage in Revelation describes this same group this way: "The dragon [Satan] was enraged with the woman, and he went to make war with the rest of her offspring, who keep the commandments of God and have the testimony of Jesus Christ." Revelation 12:17, NKJV.

The "woman" in this passage appears to be the church, the mother of "the man child," Jesus. Revelation 12:13; see also 2 Corinthians 11:2. "The rest of her offspring" (or "remnant of her seed," KJV) are those who are faithful to God at the end of time. Note especially that once again God's remnant people are identified as (a) ones who "keep the commandments of God," and (b) ones who "have the testimony of Jesus."

While it is true that much of the Christian world has

rejected the idea of obedience to God, at least three passages* in Revelation state that God's last-day Christians will be commandment-keeping people.

One cannot but wonder about this emphasis on obedience to God's commandments. Can it, perhaps, help us identify the mark of the beast mentioned in the warning of the third angel (Revelation 14:9)?

Obedience to God

Remember that John follows the third angel's warning about the mark of the beast by saying that God's true people (which he calls "saints") "keep *the commandments of God*" (Revelation 14:12)—a sort of contrasting description.

Is it possible that the mark of the beast involves disobedience to God? Do those who get the mark of the beast openly break one of God's commandments?

Daniel the prophet warned that a power would arise after the fall of the Roman empire that would "think to change times and laws." Daniel 7:25. When we look at the church that seems to fit the symbol of Babylon, we find Roman Catholic leaders and theologians claiming that the Roman Catholic Church changed God's law by changing the day of rest from Saturday to Sunday, then made all the Christian nations of the world obey *their* version.

Note the following statements from Roman Catholic sources:

"Q. Which is the Sabbath day?

"A. Saturday is the Sabbath day.

"Q. Why do we observe Sunday instead of Saturday?

"A. We observe Sunday instead of Saturday be-

---

*See Revelation 22:14, KJV, for the third passage.

cause the Catholic Church transferred the solemnity from Saturday to Sunday."—Peter Geiermann, *The Convert's Catechism of Catholic Doctrine* (1957 edition), p. 50.

"Nowhere in the Bible do we find that Christ or the apostles ordered that the Sabbath be changed from Saturday to Sunday. We have the commandment of God given to Moses to keep holy the Sabbath Day, that is the 7th day of the week, Saturday. Today most Christians keep Sunday because it has been revealed to us by the [Catholic] Church outside the Bible."—*The Catholic Virginian*, October 3, 1947.

"Q. Have you any other way of proving that the [Catholic] Church has power to institute festivals of precept?

"A. Had she not such power, she could not have done that in which all modern religionists agree with her;—she could not have substituted the observance of Sunday the first day of the week, for the observance of Saturday the seventh day, a change for which there is no Scriptural authority."—Stephen Keenan, *A Doctrinal Catechism* (3d American ed., rev.; New York: T. W. Strong, Edward Dunigan & Bro., 1876), p. 174.

A check of church history regarding the origin of Sunday sacredness substantiates the basic claim of Catholicism that the Roman church early adopted Sunday, and through her growing influence and authority brought this worship day into the habits and practices of virtually all of Christendom by the mid-sixth century A.D.

The Roman Emperor Constantine made Sunday an official secular holiday in A.D. 321. Then in A.D. 538, the Roman Catholic council known as the Third Council of Orleans issued a church law ordering that on Sunday labor be laid aside in order that all might attend church.—See C. Mervyn Maxwell, *God Cares,* vol. 1, pp. 129, 130.

The Roman Catholic Church not only admits responsibility for tampering with the law of God, but claims that Protestants who observe Sunday are paying homage to Catholicism:

"If Protestants would follow the Bible, they should worship God on the Sabbath Day. In keeping Sunday they are following a law of the Catholic Church."—Albert Smith (Chancellor of the Catholic Archdiocese of Baltimore), replying for the Cardinal in a letter of February 10, 1920.

"It was the Catholic Church which, by the authority of JESUS CHRIST, has transferred this [Sabbath] rest to the Sunday in remembrance of the resurrection of our Lord. Thus the observance of Sunday by the Protestants is an homage they pay, in spite of themselves, to the authority of the [Catholic] church."—Louis Gaston de Segur, *Plain Talk About the Protestantism of Today* (Boston: Patrick Donahoe, 1868), p. 225.

It seems that the papacy considers the power to change one of God's laws a *mark*, or evidence, of her authority in religious matters. In so doing, the church has moved into the position of God Himself and has exercised authority which rightly belongs only to the Creator-God.

The Final Crisis

In Revelation the apostle John says that just prior to the second advent of Christ—as probation for the human race draws to a close—an "image of the beast" will be formed and that it will be instrumental in enforcing the mark of the beast upon the inhabitants of earth. The threats imposed will be first, economic penalties (no one may buy or sell), then finally a death sentence on all who dare to challenge its viability. See Revelation 13:11-18.

As the activities take place to enforce the mark of the beast, the third angel's message will resound even louder, warning of the fearsome judgments which await those who accept the mark. With this thought in mind the third angel's message as preached today is a warning of issues to come, a warning that will force attention on the issue of obeying the Creator-God or an earthly substitute for God.

Since the papacy through the ages has been both a religious and a political system, it is easy to conclude that the image of the beast will also be a church-state union of some kind.

More and more Bible scholars who specialize in prophecy anticipate from the warnings of Revelation 13 and 14 that many Christian denominations, uniting on a core of commonly held beliefs and developing connections with key elements of political power, will one day become strong enough to enforce their common religious convictions by civil law—particularly the commonly held observance of Sunday, which, as we have seen, the papacy regards as a sign or identifying mark of her authority.

This interpretation explains why Revelation 14, in a sentence that comes immediately before the passage about the Son of man reaping the earth (verses 14-16), points our attention in contrast to God's last-day "saints" as "they that keep the commandments of God, and the faith of Jesus" (verse 12).

The Sabbath of the Ten Commandments will be the controversial point—the seventh day of the week that was intended to remind us of a Creator-God. As economic penalties are imposed upon those who disobey the laws of the land, the crisis will deepen. Thousands who paid little attention to God's commands and authority will have to give very earnest thought to the issues. Will they obey God's commandments or accept the mark of the beast? How will they respond to God's three final warnings? How will you and I respond? Will we follow God's simple directions for salvation—to trust His promises and obey His commands, thus opening the life to His abiding presence and His miracle-working power?

Satan's Time Runs Out

As Satan sees time slide through his fingers like so many grains of sand, he increases his efforts. "Woe to the inhabiters of the earth and of the sea! for the devil is come down unto you, having great wrath, *because he knoweth that he hath but a short time.*" Revelation 12:12, emphasis supplied.

In this climactic confrontation of Revelation 13 and 14, the agelong controversy that Satan instigated more than 6000 years ago challenging God's authority (see chapter 3) becomes very personal for earth's inhabitants. Whom do we obey—God or man? Who has our allegiance and our trust—Heaven or earth? Where lies the authority we choose to respect—in God's Word or in man's decrees?

"Here is the patience of the saints," John points out, "here are they that keep the commandments of God, and the faith of Jesus." Revelation 14:12.

In contemplation of the seriousness of God's final messages for planet Earth, we invite you to join the group who respond to the call of the three angels, who worship the Creator-God on His specified seventh-day Sabbath, and who flee from those religions that teach doctrines contrary to a "thus saith the Lord."

A Thousand Years of What?

Many people have their own ideas about what life will be like after Christ comes. This speculation especially applies to life during the millennium, the first 1,000 years following Christ's return.* A visit to almost any religious bookstore in America reveals that by far the largest majority of Christian books dealing with future events, if they discuss the millennium at all, describe this thousand-year period as a time of utopian perfection—without disease or hunger or crime or hardship or war, just universal peace, prosperity, and brotherhood.

Hal Lindsey in his best-selling book *There's a New World Coming* is certainly optimistic, but no more so than many others we might quote:

"The kingdom which Christ will bring and reign over will be a world marvelously beyond man's wildest dreams. . . . There will be peace and tranquillity. . . . The whole animal and vegetable worlds will be at their highest state of development. Man won't have marred it with the refuse of his selfish activities. The sky will

---

*The word *millennium*, though not found anywhere in the Bible, comes from the Latin *mille annus* (or "a thousand years") and has been used by Christians for centuries to identify the thousand-year period mentioned six times in the first seven verses of Revelation 20.

be bluer, the grass will be greener, the flowers will smell sweeter, the air will be cleaner, and man will be happier than he ever dreamed possible."—Pages 261, 262.

Another well-known author, Dr. M. R. DeHaan (founder and for twenty-seven years speaker of the "Radio Bible Class"), in his book *Coming Events in Prophecy,* paints a similarly glorious picture: "Sickness will be unknown during this blessed age of Christ's reign upon the earth. . . . There will be no hospitals, no clinics, no ambulances screaming down our streets, for there will be no sickness and no disease. . . . There will be no want, there will be no hunger, there will be no thirsting, there will be no problem of distribution, there will be no famine of any kind, but all will have enough, and all will be satisfied. . . . During this age there will be universal peace."—Pages 148-150.

Fascinating and alluring as these descriptions are, we believe they actually come short of what the home of the saved will be like after God has created everything new, as He promises to do in Revelation 21:5: "Behold, I make all things new."

There is, however, one problem, which is so important we feel we must mention it. These happy descriptions do not harmonize with what the Scriptures declare about the earth *during the millennium.* Let us take a close look at Revelation 20, and you'll see what we mean.

Revelation 20 is the Bible's key chapter on this fascinating period. In fact, it is the only chapter in the Bible that mentions the thousand years. It discusses three aspects of the millennium: what happens at its beginning, what happens during the millennium, and what happens at its end.

Beginning of the Millennium

[1] And I saw an angel come down from heaven, having the key of the bottomless pit and a great chain in his hand. [2] And he laid hold on the dragon, that old serpent, which is the Devil, and Satan, and bound him a thousand years, [3] and cast him into the bottomless pit, and shut him up, and set a seal upon him, that he should deceive the nations no more, till the thousand years should be fulfilled: and after that he must be loosed a little season.

During the Millennium

[4] And I saw thrones, and they sat upon them, and judgment was given unto them: and I saw the souls of them that were beheaded for the witness of Jesus, and for the word of God, and which had not worshipped the beast, neither his image, neither had received his mark upon their foreheads, or in their hands; and they lived and reigned with Christ a thousand years. [5] . . . This is the first resurrection. [6] Blessed and holy is he that hath part in the first resurrection: on such the second death hath no power, but they shall be priests of God and of Christ, and shall reign with him a thousand years.

End of the Millennium

[7] And when the thousand years are expired, Satan shall be loosed out of his prison, [8] and shall go out to deceive the nations which are in the four quarters of the earth, Gog and Magog, to gather them together to battle: the number of whom is as the sand of the sea. [9] And they went

up on the breadth of the earth, and compassed the camp of the saints about, and the beloved city: and fire came down from God out of heaven, and devoured them.

When Does Christ Return?

Obviously, Revelation 20 tells us some very significant details about the millennium. However, you may have noticed that it does not contain any specific reference to the second coming of Christ.

This omission has led to a good deal of discussion among theologians stretching over many centuries and producing various theories regarding how Christ's return fits into the events of the millennium.

Basically, these theories can be grouped under four major categories:

1. *Amillennialism*—the belief that there is no millennium at all, Revelation 20 being only allegorical in meaning.

2. *Dispensational Premillennialism*—the belief that Christ's return before the millennium consists of two phases: the first, Christ's secret rapture of His people, rescuing them from the tribulation that will devastate the earth; and the second, Christ's return *with* His saints to set up a millennial earthly kingdom composed of mortals (the "lost") and immortals (the "saved").

3. *Postmillennialism*—Christ returns after the millennium.

4. *Premillennialism*—Christ returns before the millennium.

Because of the limited size of this book, we cannot examine the pros and cons of each position in detail. We will say briefly why we reject three of the views, and then devote more space to explaining why we accept the fourth. We reject the first view because no in-

dication exists in Revelation 20 that the passage is allegorical. We reject the second because of what the Bible
teaches regarding the rapture theory and the Jewish
nation. See chapters 5 and 6 in this book.

We reject the third view (postmillennialism) because
it does not harmonize with the book of Revelation at
all. We accept the fourth view—that Christ returns before the millennium—because it fits agreeably with everything the Bible says about the return of Jesus and
the end of sin.

To start this study, let's note where Revelation 20,
the millennium chapter, fits into the rest of Revelation.
Look particularly at the latter verses of chapter 19,
those which immediately precede Revelation 20. (Remember, the chapter and verse divisions found in today's Bibles did not come to us from the original Bible
writers, but are additions made many centuries later
for the convenience of theologians and printers. They
are *not* inspired!)

We'll begin with chapter 19 verse 11: "I saw heaven
opened, and behold a white horse; and he that sat upon
him was called Faithful and True, and in righteousness
he doth judge and make war. His eyes were as a flame
of fire, and on his head were many crowns; and he had
a name written, that no man knew, but he himself. And
he was clothed with a vesture dipped in blood: and his
name is called The Word of God. And the armies which
were in heaven followed him upon white horses,
clothed in fine linen, white and clean. And out of his
mouth goeth a sharp sword, that with it he should smite
the nations. . . . And he hath on his vesture and on his
thigh a name written, KING OF KINGS, AND LORD
OF LORDS." Revelation 19:11-16.

According to the author of Revelation, the person
riding upon the white horse in this passage is "the

Lamb" (verses 7, 9), "The Word of God" (verse 13; see John 1:1-3, 14), and "King of kings, and Lord of lords" (see Revelation 17:14; 1 Timothy 6:15). All these names and titles refer to Christ.

In Revelation 19 John describes Christ coming to earth with the armies of heaven (verse 14) to "smite the nations" (verse 15). He battles the beast, the false prophet, and the various kings of the earth (verses 19, 20) and destroys all the wicked who are aligned with the beast (verses 20, 21).

Immediately after John describes the destruction of the beast and his followers (verses 20, 21), he begins describing the millennium (chapter 20:1-9). The narrative accounts of chapters 19 and 20 form a continuous description of a single event. We find no interruption of activity, no change of location, and no introduction of unrelated material between chapters 19 and 20.

With this in mind, we can easily prepare a brief outline of events connected with the millennium based on Revelation 19 and 20.

A Brief Summary of Events

Beginning of Millennium	Jesus returns as King of kings. Revelation 19:11-16.
	He destroys the wicked upon the earth. Revelation 19:18-21.
	Righteous dead are resurrected to life. Revelation 20:5, 6.
	Satan bound for a thousand years. Revelation 20:2.
During the Millennium	Righteous reign with Christ for a thousand years. Revelation 20:4, 6.
	Righteous involved with judgment during the thousand years. Revelation 20:4.

Rest of the dead (the wicked) remain dead. Revelation 20:5.

End of the Millennium Satan loosed and begins deceiving people. Revelation 20:7, 8.

The wicked attack God's "beloved city." Revelation 20:9.

Judgment takes place and sentences pronounced. Revelation 20:11-13.

Wicked cast into the lake of fire. Revelation 20:14, 15. See also verses 9, 10.

God makes a new heaven and a new earth. Revelation 21:1.

Note that Revelation 19 and 20, taken as a whole, unequivocally support view number four—premillennialism (that Christ returns *before* the millennium). But note also that these chapters do not support the view that the wicked will be alive on earth during the thousand years of the millennium.

What Happens When Christ Returns?

When Christ returns at the beginning of the millennium, one of the most significant events in human history takes place—the resurrection of the righteous who have gone to the grave during the past 6,000 years.

Paul describes this event with these words: "The Lord himself shall descend from heaven with a shout, with the voice of the archangel, and with the trump of God: and the dead in Christ shall rise first: then we which are alive and remain shall be caught up together with them in the clouds, to meet the Lord in the air: and so shall we ever be with the Lord. Wherefore comfort one another with these words." 1 Thessalonians 4:16-18.

Paul, in his letter to the church at Corinth, adds,

"Behold, I shew you a mystery; We shall not all sleep, but we shall all be changed, in a moment, in the twinkling of an eye, at the last trump: for the trumpet shall sound, and the dead shall be raised incorruptible, and we shall be changed. For this corruptible must put on incorruption, and this mortal must put on immortality." 1 Corinthians 15:51-53.

Jesus told His disciples that there would be two resurrections. He called one "the resurrection of life," and the other, the "resurrection of damnation." Look at Jesus' statement as recorded in John 5:28, 29: "All that are in the graves . . . shall come forth; they that have done good, unto the resurrection of life; and they that have done evil, unto the resurrection of damnation."

Paul, writing to the church in Thessalonica, adds, "The dead in Christ *shall rise*" when "the Lord himself shall descend from heaven." 1 Thessalonians 4:16.

If the resurrection of the righteous takes place at the second coming of Christ, the resurrection of the wicked must occur later, though Paul in this passage makes no mention of it.

Notice that the statements of *both* Christ and Paul give details about the resurrection that harmonize with Revelation 20: "They [God's people] lived and reigned with Christ a thousand years. But the rest of the dead lived not again until the thousand years were finished. This is the first resurrection." Verses 4, 5.

Thus the Bible says that the second resurrection, the resurrection of "the rest of the dead," occurs 1,000 years after the first resurrection—at the end of the millennium—and that it involves "they that have done evil."

There is even more evidence that the wicked are dead during the millennium. We have already seen from Revelation 19 that one of Christ's main purposes in returning, in addition to claiming His people, is to punish the wicked who are alive at that time. "The Lord cometh out of his place to punish the inhabitants of the earth for their iniquity." Isaiah 26:21.

Jeremiah, picturing the results of this destruction of the living wicked, declares, "The slain of the Lord shall be at that day from one end of the earth even unto the other end of the earth: they shall not be lamented, neither gathered, nor buried." Jeremiah 25:33.

If, as we have seen, the righteous dead are raised to life when Christ returns at the beginning of the millennium and the living wicked are destroyed, what happens next? Does Christ then establish His kingdom on earth for a thousand years?

Look again at Paul's statement about that day: "The Lord himself shall descend from heaven . . . : and the dead in Christ shall rise first: then we which are alive and remain shall be caught up together with them in the clouds, to meet the Lord in the air: *and so shall we ever be with the Lord.*" 1 Thessalonians 4:16, 17, emphasis supplied.

Just prior to His ascension to heaven, Jesus told Simon Peter, "Whither I go, thou canst not follow me now; but thou shalt follow me afterwards." John 13:36. He also said, "If I go and prepare a place for you, I will come again, and receive you unto myself; that where I am [*i.e.,* in heaven], there ye may be also." John 14:3. The saved will follow Jesus back to heaven on the great resurrection day. See also John 14:1-3; 17:24.

According to Revelation 20, the final event associated with Christ's second coming is the binding of Satan. See verses 1-3. This binding, of course, is not accomplished with physical ropes or chains. He will be bound in a prison of circumstances—the wicked having been destroyed by the brightness of Christ's return (see 2 Thessalonians 1:8; 2:8); the righteous, both living and dead, having been taken up to heaven (see John 14:1-3; 1 Thessalonians 4:16, 17); and the rest of the wicked still awaiting their resurrection at the end of the millennium (see Revelation 20:5). Who remains on earth for Satan to tempt?

What Happens During the Millennium?

John says, "I saw an angel come down from heaven, having the key of the bottomless pit and a great chain in his hand. And he laid hold on the dragon, that old serpent, which is the Devil, and Satan, and bound him a thousand years, and cast him into the bottomless pit." Revelation 20:1-3.

This bottomless pit is not some underground cavern in the center of the earth or a giant chasm elsewhere in the universe. The Greek word for *pit* is *abussos*, and this is the same word used in the Greek translation of the Old Testament (the Septuagint) for *the deep* in Genesis 1:2—a description of the surface of this world as it appeared on the first day of creation (*i.e.*, "without form, and void"). Thus Satan's home for the thousand years of the millennium will be this earth in a chaotic state, devoid of human life.

Isaiah, describing the world following Christ's return, wrote, "Behold, the Lord maketh the earth empty, and maketh it waste, and turneth it upside down, and scattereth abroad the inhabitants thereof. . . . *The land shall be utterly emptied, and utterly spoiled:* for the Lord hath spoken this word." Isaiah 24:1-3, emphasis supplied.

In another place Jeremiah, after seeing a vision from God, added, "I beheld the earth, and, lo, it was without form, and void; and the heavens, and they had no light. I beheld the mountains, and, lo, they trembled, and all the hills moved lightly. I beheld, and, lo, *there was no man,* and all the birds of the heavens were fled. I beheld, and, lo, the fruitful place was a wilderness, and *all the cities thereof were broken down at the presence of the Lord,* and by his fierce anger." Jeremiah 4:23-26, emphasis supplied.

The clause "all the cities thereof were broken down at the presence of the Lord" plainly identifies this event with the return of Christ. No other point in history could this passage describe. This happens when Jesus returns to gather His people from the earth and take them to heaven, during the tumultuous upheaval "when . . . every mountain and island [are] moved out of their places." See Revelation 6:14-17.

Some theologians I have talked with about these issues reply, "Jeremiah 4:23-26 describes the destruction of the wicked at the very end of time."

However, the very next verse voids that explanation. Jeremiah continues by declaring, "Thus hath the Lord said, The whole land shall be desolate; *yet will I not make a full end."* Jeremiah 4:27, emphasis supplied.

God cannot be describing the destruction of the wicked at the end of the millennium. The words, "yet will I not make a full end," make it impossible to apply this passage to the final destruction of all the wicked at the end of time.

Without a doubt God is describing the destruction of the wicked *before* the millennium, as portrayed in Revelation 19:17-21, at the time Christ returns to claim His saints. That is the significance of Jeremiah's warning that this destruction is not the full, or final, end of the wicked.

Thus, even as this world has been Satan's abode for the past 6,000 years (see Revelation 12:9; Job 2:1, 2), so will it be his home during the final thousand years. Satan and his evil angels will inhabit this desolate planet by themselves, with no one to tempt or deceive.

One especially perceptive writer, describing this period, says, "For a thousand years, Satan will wander to and fro in the desolate earth to behold the results of his rebellion against the law of God. During this time his sufferings are intense. Since his fall his life of unceasing activity has banished reflection; but he is now deprived of his power and left to contemplate the part which he has acted since first he rebelled against the government of heaven, and to look forward with trembling and terror to the dreadful future when he must suffer for all the evil that he has done and be punished for the sins that he has caused to be committed."— Ellen G. White, *The Great Controversy,* p. 660.

The Righteous in Heaven

Meanwhile, the righteous—as we have already seen—will have been taken by Christ to heaven. See John 14:1-3; 13:36. We might logically ask, What will the righteous do in heaven for a thousand years?

One activity that should prove exciting would likely involve visiting other portions of God's universe—perhaps even inhabited worlds similar to our own.

Also, the righteous in heaven during the millennium will be involved in some way in the work of judgment. Stated by Paul, "Do ye not know that the saints shall judge the world? and if the world shall be judged by you, are ye unworthy to judge the smallest matters? Know ye not that we shall judge angels?" 1 Corinthians 6:2, 3.

The books of record in heaven, including the book of

life (see Revelation 20:12; 21:27; 3:5; 13:8; 17:8; 22:19), will no doubt be open for individual scrutiny and examination. By checking the record of the lives of everyone about whom they may have questions, the righteous will be assured that God's decisions concerning the destiny of the wicked are totally just.

Think what it will be like to view on heaven's videotapes—or whatever recording techniques God employs—the origin of evil in heaven, before it spread to earth. To witness Satan's initial questioning of God's authority, his discussions with the heavenly angels, his work to undermine their trust, and their loyalty to His government. To behold almost firsthand the great battle in heaven between Satan and his angels and Michael and His angels. See Revelation 12:4, 7-9, 13.

By methods far beyond anything humans have even thought of, the righteous will be able to view the great struggles for human minds: Adam's, Eve's, Noah's, Abraham's, Moses', Isaiah's, Jeremiah's, and Daniel's. The righteous will witness anew Christ's incarnation, His birth, His life on earth, His trial, His crucifixion.

The righteous will watch the angel from heaven roll back the stone from in front of the tomb on that Sunday morning 2,000 years ago and see Jesus step forth in victory from the bonds of death.

The righteous will be able to see the lives, struggles, and victories of their own ancestors and—for many—their children, grandchildren, and great-grandchildren. They will be able to "view the videotapes" of the earthly lives of their ancestors and descendants and watch them as they faced the same kinds of conflicts and suffered many of the same kinds of trials as they themselves endured.

The opportunities to study the plan of salvation in

action along the lines of an ever-expanding web of interrelated human beings—both backward and forward in time—should alone provide ample material to occupy several hundred years or so. Certainly such a study can continue until each of the righteous is satisfied why various individuals did or did not make it to heaven.

That is why the righteous will sing songs like the one John heard "much people" in heaven singing: "Alleluia; Salvation, and glory, and honour, and power, unto the Lord our God: for true and righteous are his judgments." Revelation 19:1, 2.

In our next chapter we will see what takes place at the end of the millennium.

God's Great Judgment Day

As I sat down to prepare the final few pages of this book, I read an account in this morning's *Washington Post* about the execution yesterday of convicted killer Anthony Antone at 7:00 a.m. on January 26, 1984. "As 47 people watched," the story related, "Antone became the twelfth man to be executed in the United States since the death penalty ban was lifted in 1976, and the first this year." Antone died in the electric chair for his part in the gangland murder of a former policeman.

But the aspect of the story that caught my attention was that Antone went to his death in the electric chair spurning the services of a minister and rejecting Christianity itself, which he called a "childish" belief.

One can only imagine what thoughts must have gone through his mind during those final minutes as he was being strapped into the electric chair, facing death with no hope for the future.

Unfortunately for Antone and for millions of others who enter eternity unprepared, *pretending* there is no future after death (or no God, or no day of judgment, or no heaven or hellfire) doesn't make it true.

God's Word is most emphatic about future events—especially the day of judgment. "He hath appointed a day, in the which he will judge the world in righteous-

113

ness," said the apostle Paul. Elsewhere he stated, "We must all appear before the judgment seat of Christ" and "every one of us shall give account of himself to God." Acts 17:31; 2 Corinthians 5:10; Romans 14:12.

In another place we find this statement: "God shall bring every work into judgment, with every secret thing, whether it be good, or whether it be evil." Ecclesiastes 12:14.

"Every one of us," the Bible says, must face God in judgment. This even includes people like Anthony Antone, who died denying Christianity and everything related to it. It may have seemed "childish" to a convicted killer, but how trivial will it seem when Anthony and millions of others wake up and find themselves face to face with God on that great judgment day?

But we're getting ahead of our story. We need to see first how the day of judgment fits into the final events of earth's history.

In our last chapter we discovered eight things about the millennium:

1. That Christ's second coming occurs at the beginning of the millennium.

2. That Christ destroys the wicked still alive then.

3. That He raises the righteous dead to life.

4. That the righteous living and resurrected dead are taken back with Him to heaven.

5. That the rest of the dead (the wicked) remain dead.

6. That Satan and his evil angels are confined to earth by themselves for a thousand years.

7. That the earth remains in ruins during the millennium.

8. That the righteous in heaven will have a part in the judgment of earth's inhabitants.

Now let's look at the final events that occur at the end of the millennium. According to Revelation 20, "When the thousand years have expired, Satan will be released from his prison and will go out to deceive the nations which are in the four corners of the earth, . . . to gather them together to battle, whose number is as the sand of the sea. They went up on the breadth of the earth and surrounded the camp of the saints and the beloved city. And fire came down from God out of heaven and devoured them." Revelation 20:7-9, NKJV.

Two Resurrections at the End of Time

Remember in our last chapter that we discovered that the Bible refers to *two* resurrections at the end of time—one at the beginning of the millennium for the righteous (called the "resurrection of life") and a second a thousand years later for the wicked (called the "resurrection of damnation"). See John 5:28, 29; 1 Thessalonians 4:16; Revelation 20:4, 5.

This "resurrection of damnation," which occurs at the end of the millennium (Revelation 20:5), involves all the wicked of all ages. It is this vast horde of resurrected people "the number of whom is as the sand of the sea" (verse 8) that Satan sets out to deceive and to gather together for battle.

Our next question is Who does Satan plan to fight? Obviously, the saints in "the beloved city." Revelation 20:9 says that this city is on earth at the end of the millennium.

Other passages confirm that at the end of the thousand years, immediately prior to the resurrection of the wicked, Christ returns to this world with the righteous. "The Lord my God shall come, and all the saints with thee." Zechariah 14:5. "His feet shall stand in that day upon the mount of Olives, . . . and the mount of Olives shall cleave in the midst thereof toward the east and toward the west, and there shall be a very great valley." Verse 4.

Next the heavenly city, the New Jerusalem, descends upon the area purified by Christ. John describes the scene, "I John saw the holy city, new Jerusalem, coming down from God out of heaven, prepared as a bride adorned for her husband." Revelation 21:2.

This beloved city Paul describes as "a city which hath foundations, whose builder and maker is God." Hebrews 11:10; see also Hebrews 11:16; 12:22; 13:14. It is the same city that Jesus told His disciples He was going to heaven to build. See John 14:1-3.

Satan Launches an Attack

With the New Jerusalem here on earth and the wicked of all ages resurrected back to life, Satan feels confident that by sheer force of numbers he can successfully overcome Christ at last. Here's how one writer describes the scene: "Now Satan prepares for a last mighty struggle for the supremacy. While deprived of his power [during the millennium] and cut off from his work of deception, the prince of evil was miserable and dejected; but as the wicked dead are raised and he sees the vast multitudes upon his side, his hopes revive, and he determines not to yield the great controversy. He will marshall all the armies of the lost under his banner and through them endeavor to execute his plans.

"The wicked are Satan's captives. In rejecting Christ they have accepted the rule of the rebel leader. They are ready to receive his suggestions and to do his bidding. Yet, true to his early cunning, he does not acknowledge himself to be Satan. He claims to be the prince who is the rightful owner of the world and whose inheritance has been unlawfully wrested from him.

"He represents himself to his deluded subjects as a redeemer, assuring them that his power has brought them forth from the graves and that he is about to rescue them from the most cruel tyranny. . . . He proposes to lead them against the camp of the saints and to take possession of the City of God. With fiendish exultation he points to the unnumbered millions who have been raised from the dead and declares that as their leader he is well able to overthrow the city and regain his throne and his kingdom."—Ellen G. White, *The Great Controversy*, p. 663.

Revelation 20:9, NKJV, says, "They went up on the breadth of the earth and surrounded the camp of the saints and the beloved city. And fire came down from God out of heaven and devoured them."

Judgment Is Pronounced Upon the Wicked

Satan's futile attack upon the New Jerusalem is the final act of rebellion in the great galactic battle between Christ and Satan. In this final drama, the entire human race from the first human to the last meets for the first and last time. Inside the city the redeemed of all ages stand with their Saviour, Jesus. Outside the walls the lost of all ages stand with their leader, Satan.

As the wicked begin their attack, God halts them in their tracks and convenes the eternal court. John describes the event:

"I saw a great white throne, and him that sat on it, from whose face the earth and the heaven fled away; and there was found no place for them. And I saw the dead, small and great, stand before God; and the books were opened: and another book was opened, which is the book of life: and the dead were judged out of those things which were written in the books, according to their works. . . . And they were judged every man according to their works." Revelation 20:11-13.

The "dead" that John describes are not disembodied spirits, but resurrected humans. "The sea gave up the dead which were in it; and death and hell [the grave] delivered up the dead which were in them: and they were judged every man." Revelation 20:13.

Another writer describes this event with these words: "The Lord cometh with ten thousands of his saints, to execute judgment upon all, and to convince all that are ungodly among them of all their ungodly deeds which they have ungodly committed, and of all their hard speeches which ungodly sinners have spoken against him." Jude 14, 15.

Note particularly the phrase "to execute judgment." This is in keeping with what we have already said about the saints taking part in the process of judgment during the millennium in heaven. When the wicked stand before God in judgment, God plans to execute His sentences upon the wicked. The sentences have already been studied in detail by all the redeemed. Now it is time for the wicked to hear the verdicts, each one his own verdict.

What will be the results of this day of judgment? The Bible tells us that "we shall all stand before the judgment seat of Christ. For it is written, As I live, saith the Lord, *every knee shall bow to me, and every tongue shall confess to God*." Romans 14:10, 11, emphasis supplied. And in another place, we read the same, "All they that go down to the dust [i.e., the dead who will be resurrected] shall bow down before him." Psalm 22:29.

When the wicked of all history stand in judgment before Christ, they will see that the outcome of their sins is inevitable. They will recognize that they are unfit to enter the Holy City of God. And in acknowledgment of this fact, they bow together before Christ and willingly, publicly praise His divinity and the justice of His sentence. "God also hath highly exalted him, and given him a name which is above every name: that at the name of Jesus every knee should bow, of things in heaven, and things in earth. . . ; and that every tongue should confess that Jesus Christ is Lord." Philippians 2:9-11.

Even the archenemy himself, Satan, will fall on the ground prostrate before Jesus. Speaking symbolically to the king of Tyrus, God's inspired writer described Satan's rebellion. See Ezekiel 28:12-19. He declared, "Thine heart was lifted up because of thy beauty, thou hast corrupted thy wisdom by reason of thy brightness: *I will cast thee to the ground*, I will lay thee before kings, that they may behold thee." Ezekiel 28:17, emphasis supplied. (Since this passage describes this being as having been "in Eden" and "upon the holy mountain of God," and since it identifies him as having been an angel in heaven—see verses 13 and 14—we know that it has valid application to Satan and not merely to an earthly king. See the more complete discussion in chapter 2, "Does Satan Really Exist?")

God Destroys the Wicked

John, describing what will happen to the wicked after sentence is pronounced upon them, states, "Fire came down from God out of heaven, and devoured them" "and whosoever was not found written in the book of life was cast into the lake of fire." Revelation 20:9, 15.

Not only does this fire destroy the wicked, it also

burns up every trace of man's activities over the past 6,000 years. "The day of the Lord will come. . . ; in the which the heavens shall pass away with a great noise, and the elements shall melt with fervent heat, *the earth also and the works that are therein shall be burned up.* Seeing then that all these things shall be dissolved, what manner of persons ought ye to be in all holy conversation and godliness?" 2 Peter 3:10, 11, emphasis supplied. "The Lord cometh forth out of his place, and will come down, and tread upon the high places of the earth. And the mountains shall be molten under him, and the valleys shall be cleft, as wax before the fire." Micah 1:3, 4.

Obviously, this fire will annihilate the wicked—it actually reduces them to ashes.

"The day cometh, that shall burn as an oven; and all the proud, yea, and all that do wickedly, shall be stubble: and the day that cometh shall burn them up, saith the Lord of hosts, that it shall leave them neither root nor branch. . . . And ye shall tread down the wicked; for they *shall be ashes under the soles of your feet in the day that I shall do this*, saith the Lord of hosts." Malachi 4:1-3, emphasis supplied.

In this terrible fire, Satan will die. See Ezekiel 28:18, 19. The destruction will be complete, and rebellion will never again arise. "What do ye imagine against the Lord? he will make an utter end: affliction shall not rise up the second time." Nahum 1:9. Sin and sinners will never again exist in the universe: "Let the sinners be consumed out of the earth, and let the wicked be no more." Psalm 104:35.

In our final chapter we will discover what God has planned for our world following its cleansing by fire and, more important, how we can personally prepare to meet Christ when He returns.

An Earth Made New

"Human language is inadequate to describe the reward of the righteous. It will be known only to those who behold it. No finite mind can comprehend the glory of the Paradise of God."—Ellen G. White.

While it is true that the Bible describes a rather dim future for the world as we have known it, God's Word does not end with this negative description.

Look at what Peter wrote: "We, according to his promise, look for new heavens and a new earth, wherein dwelleth righteousness." 2 Peter 3:13.

"And I saw a new heaven and a new earth," wrote John, "for the first heaven and the first earth were passed away." Revelation 21:1.

Nothing will remain in the earth made new to remind us of this sinful, sick world—except the crucifixion scars in Christ's hands and feet (see John 20:20, 25, 27; Luke 24:38-40), which apparently He will bear throughout eternity.

This earth made new will become our eternal home. See Matthew 5:5. It will also be the dwelling place of God: "I heard a great voice out of heaven saying, Behold, the tabernacle of God is with men, and he will dwell with them, and they shall be his people, and God himself shall be with them, and be their God. And God shall wipe away all tears from their eyes; and there shall be no more death, neither sorrow, nor crying, neither shall there be any more pain: for the former things are passed away." Revelation 21:3, 4.

Not only will our physical world experience a dramatic change, but the conditions of Eden prior to the Fall will be restored—with no climatic extremes, no floods, no earthquakes, and no pollution or smog.

The blight of sickness that so often attacks humans today will be utterly banished. Those who through accident, disease, or birth have spent a lifetime in blindness; or whose ears have never heard the laughter of a child, the song of birds, or the music of an orchestra; or who have no legs of their own to run and walk will have these faculties restored. "Then the eyes of the blind shall be opened, and the ears of the deaf shall be unstopped. Then shall the lame man leap as an hart, and the tongue of the dumb sing." Isaiah 35:5, 6.

Too many spiritualize away what life will be like in eternity (and thus we see cartoons showing people with wings sitting on clouds playing golden harps). "Eye hath not seen, nor ear heard, neither have entered into the heart of man," Paul says, "the things which God hath prepared for them that love him." 1 Corinthians 2:9. God's earth made new will be a place of fun, excitement, joy, and unending adventure for the redeemed.

But there is one hitch. As we have sorrowfully seen in chapters 9 and 11, not every human will have a part in that new life. Some will have deliberately chosen not to. Peter, in the passage we quoted at the beginning of this chapter, also said, "Since all these things will be dissolved, what manner of persons ought you to be in holy conduct and godliness, looking for and hastening the coming of the day of God?" 2 Peter 3:11, 12, NKJV.

God can save only those who accept His generous offer of salvation. In Romans 3:23 we discover that "all have sinned, and come short of the glory of God." That means that *all of us* face a certain death sentence, worse than did Anthony Antone whom we mentioned in the previous chapter.

Fortunately, though, the Bible provides a way of escape. Although Romans 6:23 declares that "the wages of sin is death," it goes on to assure us that "the gift of God is eternal life through Jesus Christ our Lord." God does not want us to die, so He has provided a way of escape. "And this is the record, that God hath given to us eternal life, *and this life is in his Son. He that hath the Son hath life*; and he that hath not the Son of God hath not life." 1 John 5:11, 12, emphasis supplied.

These words harmonize perfectly with a statement Jesus Himself made while on earth: "He that heareth my word, and believeth on him that sent me, hath everlasting life, and shall not come into condemnation; but is passed from death unto life." John 5:24.

An Offer We Cannot Refuse

How simple and uncomplicated God makes salvation! With what compassion He entreats us to make the right choice! Accept God's pardon, opening your life to His indwelling presence and control, and enjoy eternity in an earth made new, with the whole universe to explore in your spare time. "Why will ye die?" He pleads. Ezekiel 18:31. Spurn the offer, or treat it as "childish" and insignificant, and He must give you up to Satan and all the lost in the lake of fire, which was not prepared for you, but only "for the devil and his angels." Matthew 25:41.

Soon it will be too late. Regarding the fulfillment of the various signs discussed in chapters 7 and 8, Jesus said, "When ye shall see all these things, know that it is near, even at the doors." Matthew 24:33.

Yes, Jesus is coming soon. This is how the world will end. Jesus offers us hope beyond the frightening headlines. As you look at the outstretched hands of Him who offers eternal life, notice the nailprints there. He suffered for you, He died for you, so that every awful judgment you have discovered in this book will not fall on you. All you need to do is say, "Yes, Lord, I seek forgiveness. I seek salvation. By Your grace I will walk in Your ways. Adopt me into Your heavenly family. Make me Yours and transform me into a new man, a new woman, a new young person."

My sincere prayer, dear reader, is that we can meet each other personally in that wonderful earth made new. Let's plan on it.

Something for you . . .

☐ Send me a free copy of *Signs of the Times*, the international prophetic monthly.

☐ Enroll me in one of your free Bible courses.

☐ I want information about the Five-Day Plan to Stop Smoking.

☐ I would like more information about the Bible prophecies of Daniel and Revelation.

☐ Send me the address of the nearest Adventist church.

☐ I would like to know more about Seventh-day Adventists and what they believe.

Complete the coupon below, and mail to

Pacific Press Publishing Association
P.O. Box 7000, Boise, ID 83707

_____

Name

_____

Street or Box

_____

City   State   Zip

For faster service call:
Alaska or Hawaii
  call toll free: 800-253-3002
Michigan call collect: 616-471-3522
Others call toll free: 800-253-7077

Something for you . . .

☐ Send me a free copy of *Signs of the Times*, the international prophetic monthly.

☐ Enroll me in one of your free Bible courses.

☐ I want information about the Five-Day Plan to Stop Smoking.

☐ I would like more information about the Bible prophecies of Daniel and Revelation.

☐ Send me the address of the nearest Adventist church.

☐ I would like to know more about Seventh-day Adventists and what they believe.

Complete the coupon below, and mail to

Pacific Press Publishing Association
P.O. Box 7000, Boise, ID 83707

_____

Name

_____

Street or Box

_____

City   State   Zip

For faster service call:
Alaska or Hawaii
  call toll free: 800-253-3002
Michigan call collect: 616-471-3522
Others call toll free: 800-253-7077